Breaking Through Barriers

Volume 2

A collection of short stories from powerful, courageous, and determined women

Presented by Author:

Tanicia

"Shamay Speaks"

Currie

Published by Shamay Speaks www.ShamaySpeaks.com

Book cover designed by Shauny B with KnockSmith Productions www.knocksmithmagazine.com

Printed in the United States of America

ISBN: 978-0-9966729-2-4

Dedication

I dedicate this book to all the women who have stepped out of their comfort zone and taken a chance, by following their dreams. I also dedicate this book to the single mothers out there who never give up on their goals. I thank all the women who believed in me to lead them during their journey to authorship. I truly appreciate every courageous woman that has allowed me to coach and assist them in accomplishing their goal and sharing their story.

Synopsis:

Breaking Through Barriers Volume 2 is a collection of short stories from powerful, courageous, and determined women who are ready to spread their message. This book features amazing women from different walks of life, who have gained strength and wisdom from their past, while learning to move forward. The book's visionary, Tanicia "Shamay Speaks" Currie, believes that God has the power to turn your "mess" into a MESSage and that we all have a story that can provide someone with insight, inspiration, and motivation. Being a four-time author herself, Tanicia believes that sharing your story can be the first step to healing and overcoming your past experiences as she feels her first published book served as her therapy process. Always have faith in knowing you can break through any barriers life presents.

About the Visionary Tanicia "Shamay Speaks" Currie:

Tanicia "Shamay Speaks" Currie is a single mother with a full time job, who does not believe in settling in life. Having faced many life challenges, including having three heart surgeries in just 32 years, Tanicia feels that God definitely gave her a purpose. Growing up in a challenging environment with a drug addiction in her home, she convinced herself that there had to be more to life than those circumstances. Rather than allow her upbringing to dictate her success, she decided to turn her life's hardships into motivation to persevere in life. She became the first in her immediate family to graduate college with a Bachelor's degree. In 2009, she went on to open Cause' N A Stir Entertainment, hosting events from concerts to fashion shows to annual toy drives. Her life changed in 2013 when her daughter Laniyah was born. Laniyah is the best blessing she ever received, but becoming a mother also showed her that it was time to kick life into overdrive. Tanicia is currently the CEO of Branches of Community Services, which helps her give back to those in need. In 2014, she decided to finish the book she started over 8 years prior. She published her first book titled *"Deep Within I Knew He Wasn't for Me* in October 2015. Tanicia is a featured author in two empowerment books *Igniting The Vision* and *Stand Up Be*

Heard. She is the visionary behind a book compilation titled *"Breaking Through Barriers"* Vol 1 which released July 2016. Tanicia is currently working with 12 amazing women, assisting them with accomplishing their dream of becoming published authors, these lovely ladies are featured in Tanicia's compilation titled "Breaking Through Barriers" Vol 2 releasing January 2017. Her next book will release early 2017. Being passionate about empowering others to rise above their circumstances and take charge of their destiny, Tanicia's mission in life is to chase all that life has to offer, never give up, and stay humble. Tanicia truly hopes to use her life story, books, videos, events, and speaking to inspire others to follow their dreams despite their circumstances. Tanicia's theme for 2017 is "Purpose, Progress, and Moving Forward!" Tanicia looks forward to leaving an empowering legacy for her daughter, as well as, enjoying the extraordinary journey that God has laid out for her!

Tanicia "Shamay Speaks" Currie Mission:

I am often asked what do you do? Here's my answer which is my mission:

"I assist and support women in discovering their potential in life while understanding that they deserve the BEST in Life, Business, and Relationships"

Fun facts about Shamay: Shamay loves to speak on real life topics and relationships. Check out her weekly videos and topics on Facebook and Youtube.

Subscribe To Shamay's Channel:

www.youtube.com/shamayspeaks

Follow Shamay:

www.facebook.com/shamayspeaks

Instagram & twitter @shamayspeaks

Email: shamayspeaks@gmail.com

Table of Contents

Introduction

I truly feel the messages in this amazing book speak for themselves, but I wanted to start the book with these tips I have learned thus far from *Breaking Barriers Voume 1:*

12 Life and Success Tips:

1) Know your worth and understand that you deserve the BEST in life, business, and relationships. Worth translates into your confidence.

2) No matter what you have been through, no matter your upbringing, it does not define you.

3) Set a goal to be better than you were yesterday. Change doesn't happen overnight and neither does healing past hurts. So be very careful to not let your past outshine your future.

4) Being broke is a mindset. Also remember some people have broken mindsets so they will not understand your vision and that's okay!

5) Be unapologetic about your success and accomplishments; don't dim your light for anyone.

6) Baby steps are fine. Remember a step not taken is an opportunity missed.

7) As Caterina Rando says, "DONE is better than perfect." So be willing to just go for it and learn as you go. Life is trial and error.

8) To be successful, you must be willing to sacrifice and step out your of comfort zone. There's rarely success with staying in your comfort zone.

9) Seek a mentor or life/business coach. Yes, getting help and support is okay because if you could have done it alone, you would have done it by now.

10) Actions speak louder than words; don't be a talker, be a doer!

11) The only failures are quitters so you will never know your potential if you quit before you begin.

12) As my Pastors Shantell and Damon Owens said, "be a frog not a grasshopper." Grasshoppers stay in the grass, frogs leap; so are you going to stay stuck in the grass like a grasshopper or leap into your destiny?

Remember the world is waiting for your story!

Discovering

And

Pursuing My

Purpose

"Breaking Through Barriers" Visionary

How will your story be written?

By

Author Tanicia "Shamay Speaks" Currie

Author ~ Event Planner/Host ~ Entrepreneur ~ Coach

Age 34

Pittsburg, CA

www.ShamaySpeaks.com

Find me on Facebook, Instagram, Google+, and more

Your Story Leads To Your Purpose:

I start by asking, do you know how your story is being written? Do you control your destiny or do you live in fear, allowing your dreams to pass you by? Think about that as you read. You know if anyone had asked me at age 16, 20, or even 28, if I thought I would be an author one day, I would probably have said, "I am not sure." Here I am today, at age 34 and I am a four-time author who is currently working on her 2nd book compilation. I am working with thirteen amazing women featured in this book compilation, as well as, hosting monthly self-publishing workshops and more. Who would have known that those four pages I wrote over nine years ago would become part of my 1st book. I have written about some of my life experiences in Igniting the Vision, Stand Up Be Heard, and my 1st book Deep Within I Knew; however, for this chapter I want to discuss how I realized I was walking in my purpose, as well as, how I refuse to let anything stop me. The old saying, "you control your destiny," is something I firmly believe. I also believe in not allowing circumstances to dictate your success and progress. During the time I was working on those books, I knew my story was still being written. It's interesting because I honestly didn't think of my life as a story, at first, because I just viewed it as life being life. We tend to think life is just life, especially when life is just always happening to us. We don't think that our story can be a message to help or encourage someone, especially when our lives are in chaos.

I started to title this chapter, "Single mother, so what" because I wanted to go in that direction being that I am a single mother of a beautiful 3 ½ year old daughter. Becoming a mother, let alone a single mother, was one of my biggest life changes. My reason for wanting that title is because I have seen many mothers, including my own, allow their story to be more struggle than triumph. I have actually seen a few mothers use being a single mother as an excuse for their poor choices, poor parenting, and lack of success. I am in no way, shape, or form trying to say that single parenthood is easy because that would be furthest from the truth. I will say what single parenthood is not; it is not a disability. Does single parenthood makes things harder? Yes it does, but we cannot allow that circumstance to disable our ability to rise above and be successful. I know the struggle of being a single parent, especially with a single income and no reliable child support. It is not easy at all. I also know that the stress alone of being a single parent, with no help, can break you down, if you allow it to. The stress can be even worse if, on top of all that, you are dealing with a bunch of unnecessary drama. During those times, you must be steadfast in your faith and also know that what was meant to break you will make you stronger. As single mothers, we cannot allow that fact alone to dictate our story and how it's written. It is only part of our story, not the end of it.

I had been an entrepreneur after college for almost three years before I had my daughter and became a single mother. My experience of becoming a mother was enough to write a book about, hence my 1st book *"Deep Within I Knew He Wasn't For Me."* Not only was I becoming a single mother, I truly felt like my dream and longing for a family was crushed. My goal to have the family I never had was crushed and my heart was crushed. You definitely have to get the book to further understand what I experienced. As a single mother, I feel that many of us may become discouraged and forget the fact that we deserve the BEST in life despite our circumstances. The most important thing I realized about that whole ordeal was that I was not valuing myself. I firmly believe that knowing your self-worth ties into more than self-love, because it can affect your goals and relationships. I realized I wasn't valuing my worth in business either. I really went through a funk and I took a break from business. During that break, I had to reevaluate my life and what I learned was that I was not valuing myself like I should. If you think deeply about it, you can see how self-worth affects more than one area of your life. Not valuing your worth can affect your relationships because you may allow others to mistreat you, and much more. Not valuing your self-worth can affect your goals and dreams because you may feel as if you don't deserve success or you can fall a victim to allowing others' opinions to dictate your success. Overall, not valuing your self-worth can affect your life, period, because it can keep the door open for the devil to win. The devil comes in the form of self-defeating thoughts, fear, doubt, obstacles, and much more. Always remember this scripture, *"The thief cometh not, but for to steal, and to kill, and to destroy: I am come that they might have life, and that they might have [it] more abundantly." (King James Version*, John 10:10). Although I was not valuing my self-worth, I learned from it. It has become part of my story, which translates into part of my message, so I have no regrets anymore. The less you love yourself, the more the devil wins. So will you allow him to steal your future?

FEAR Disables You:

Again, I ask, how is your story being written? Is life just happening to you? Or are you full of fear? Is fear stopping you from starting that business you always dreamed of? Or is fear stopping you from telling your story and writing that book you always talk about? It has been said that F. E. A. R. is False Evidence Appearing Real or Face Everything And Rise. Fear always shows up no matter what you have going on in life. Fear is not the problem but what you do with fear is. What makes you who you are is being able to move past fear. Know and understand this, as soon as you set out to pursue your dreams, the devil gets busier. As I stated earlier, fear appears in the form of self-defeating thoughts, self-doubt, procrastination, and even negative people. Associating with negative people can bring on fear because they don't see your vision. Those negative people can plant a seed of fear in you or contribute to the negative thoughts you may have had. It is important to surround yourself with like-minded people who support your vision and encourage you; this means you may have to take inventory of those around you. Remember nothing of value comes easy; so be sure to not allow the devil to win with fear. The devil increases your fear, it's like he works overtime to disable you from following your dreams. Time is of the essence, don't wallow or linger in fear or discouragement for long. Know that you, without a doubt, will have moments of discouragement; understand that this is normal. Crush fear by taking consistent steps towards your dreams, along with having faith and praying. If you continue living in fear, you'll never get to see the value you and your story holds.

Mind Your Mindset:

As my great friend and author, Kanishia Wallace said in *Breaking Through Barriers, Vol. 1*, we must "mind our mindsets". Now ain't that the truth? This means we have to be in charge of our mindsets and check ourselves sometimes. From minding your mindset, create a "high road habit" as I call it, especially if you have a lot of baggage to work though. Baggage can hold you back and steal your joy, if you let it. When creating a happiness habit or a high road habit, keep in mind that developing a high road habit is NOT an overnight process. It is about the results you get while learning and growing from the process. The high road habit clears unnecessary drama from your life, which in essence, gives you more clarity to focus on your dreams. The less clarity you have, the more the devil replaces your dreams with fear. Once I did this, I gained more clarity by freeing myself from the feeling that I had to react to all the people and things the devil threw my way. Working on having a "high road habit" while minding my mindset is where my sanity lies.

Even simple work on your mindset causes you to gain more clarity to walk in your purpose. The more clarity your mind experiences, the more you have a clear vision of what you deserve in life, as well as, truly seeing your capabilities. Get your mind right and don't let the devil rule your life, take charge of your story and your life. Yea, I am being urban when I tell you to stop letting the devil punk you! Stop letting him punk your peace of mind and the greatness right out of you.

When pursuing your purpose you must be working towards having a strong peace of mind and knowing your happy place. Peace of mind is also what you gain from minding your mindset. When you have peace of mind, you have less fear and less uncertainty.

When you set out to pursue what God promised you, it requires faith. It doesn't require you to dwell on painful pasts or mistakes. The enemy is working overtime especially when you are setting yourself up for greatness.

Read these scriptures:

Romans 8:28: *And we know that in all things God works for the good of those who love him, who have been called according to his purpose.*

Romans 12:2: *Do not conform to the pattern of this world, but be transformed by the renewing of your mind. Then you will be able to test and approve what God's will is—his good, pleasing and perfect will. (http://biblehub.com/romans/12-2.htm)*

Lastly, my 2016 theme is *Speak Upward, Shift Upward*, this means to make it a habit of speaking positivity over your life, people in your life, and your circumstances.

Step Out Into Your Purpose:

There is no success with staying in your comfort zone or with being complacent. Staying in your comfort zone is like being stopped at a stop sign waiting for it to turn green, as if it's a stoplight. Get it? In your comfort zone lies fear, but consistency builds your faith, not just in yourself, but faith that you can change lives starting with your own. Had I allowed fear to keep me stuck then I would have never been able to accomplish the great things I have. Will you step out on faith or be a part of the crowd?

Success, Purpose, and Confirmations:

Now I've talked about minding your mindset, having peace of mind, and the "highroad habit". You must begin to do those things in order to have clarity. Start to do these things today. As they say, "there is no time like the present." Remember, a great way to be sure to see your confirmations is to do the following: mindset your mindset, practice the "high road habit" with negative situations, and gain clarity from your peace of mind. My story is how I walked into discovering my purpose, but my message led to me actually seeing my purpose. Your clear mindset and faith allows you to see your confirmations.

My confirmations have come in many forms, such as a blessing coming my way, people being placed in my life, or even just doors opening. When you start to see your purpose manifest, it's a great feeling and it's something that money can't buy. Growing up, resentment served as my motivation. But, that is no longer the case. I now appreciate my past because it shaped me. My life has purpose as I assist other beautiful women in pursuing their purpose. I understand that I am just a step in the stairs to their destiny but I feel extremely blessed to be that step. The amazing women I work with are part of God's confirmation that I walk in purpose.

Confirmations assist you in understanding your purpose but you must have faith to see and fully understand these confirmations. God aligned my confirmations for me. I believe they led me to continue writing my story, which was me walking in my purpose.

You see, I had done many things, such as modeling, a Youtube talk show, concerts, and more; however, some of my greatest joy in business didn't come until years later. What I can say is, I never quit. Because as they say, "the only failures are quitters!"

Growing up, I often think about how many people have told me things like, "You talk too much." or "You always got something to say." yet now my talking has purpose so I'm no longer offended by the words of others. You see I am a total extrovert and I used to apologize for my outspokenness at times, but no longer. I am not here to seek anyone's approval and I no longer give a crap (excuse my French) what people think because God is my judge, not man. I will not be discouraged by others' opinions because I am a confident woman walking in God's ordered steps. Even those comments people made to me about "talking too much" were confirmations because I speak with purpose. Reflect on past confirmations you may have missed.

Always remember that you possess the power each day to change the way your story has been written up until that day. So I ask you to really ask yourself how your story will be written. As long as you're breathing your story is still being written. It's like your life is an antique typewriter and every key you press is a step you take in life. Like an antique typewriter, there is no backspace button, so you can't change your past; however, you can continue typing and shift your story in a different direction. Like my coach, Sheya Chisenga, once said, "You can always make more money but you can never make more time." Don't waste your time thinking about your dreams; spend your time pursuing them, no matter what. You write your story with every step you take, choice, or decision you make. Write the best story possible even if that story is a rollercoaster. Just roll with the punches, while maintaining your peace of mind and faith. Reflect on everything I just spoke on and go on writing your story with the best you got!

You have nothing to lose, but everything to gain by taking a step out on faith into your purpose.

Here are two scriptures to leave you with:

2 Corinthians 5:17 *Therefore, if anyone is in Christ, the new creation has come: The old has gone, the new is here! (New International Version)*

Philippians 4:13 *(New King James Version)*

I can do all things through Christ who strengthens me

Write your BEST story!

Shamay Speaks vision/mission: *"I assist and support women in discovering their potential in life while understanding that they deserve the BEST in Life, Business, and Relationships"*

The Journey to Completing My Purpose

By

Anita Davis McAllister

Age 58

Author ~ Child Care Teacher ~ Speaker ~ Praise Dancer

Spoken Word Ministry

Email: spokenwordministry4@gmail.com

Pittsburg, CA

Who am I? That is a question most people ask themselves when they are trying to discover who they are and what their purpose in life is. I am Anita Davis McAllister and I am 58 years old. I was born in Detroit, Michigan and raised in Pittsburg, California. I am the founder of Spoken Word Ministry and Aminah's Spoken Word. I am also a worship dancer. This is who I am now, but my past tells a story of someone different. My past says that I was a person who was an emotional wreck. My life was an emotional roller coaster. I was confused at times with what was going on in my life. How was I going to make it being a single mother and handle the struggles that came with it. The emotional weight was so hard to bear that there were times when I cried out of frustration and brokenness; I experienced anxiety attacks and depression. Nobody knew what was going on with me because I hid it well. I put a smile on my face as if everything was good. No one knew the emotional torture that was going on inside of me; I felt misused, mistreated, and unloved. I was talked about and lied on and all of that broke my spirit. What I was going through at that time reminds me of the saying, "Don't judge a book by its cover". Even though I looked fine on the outside, in reality, on the inside I was slowly breaking down.

Let's start from the beginning. I am the mother of four children - one daughter, age 36 and three sons, ages 34, 30 and 18. They were a gift from God and I love them with my whole heart. I am blessed to have them in my life. At the age of sixteen, I met my first husband; he was two years older than me. He was in the army and when he came back home on leave in 1978 we decided to get married. We were married on December 28, 1978, a week before my 21st birthday. Within the first year of marriage, I had my first child, my only daughter. During my marriage to my first husband we moved around a lot due to him being in the army. We moved every three years from Tacoma, Washington to Bellville, Michigan then to Honolulu, Hawaii. Before we moved to Hawaii, I had my second child. During our stay in Hawaii, our marriage started falling apart and we couldn't work things out. So three months after having my third child, my husband and I separated and I moved me and my three kids back to Pittsburg, California. The failure of this marriage caused my heart to break; I began to close my heart off to certain people. I needed to heal but the problem was I didn't know how. I didn't know how to forgive and I didn't know that these feelings would follow me into my next two marriages.

My children and I moved in with my mom and my step dad. With our new living situation, I was more than determined to be the best mom I could be. After living with my parents for a year, I was able to find a home for my family. My two oldest were in school and my youngest was in day care so this allowed me to work part time and to go to school part time. I was also able to be at home with my kids at night. Being a single mom wasn't easy; it came with its struggles. I worked various jobs just to make ends meet. At one point I was working two jobs just to put food on the table and clothes on my kid's backs. It wasn't easy working more than one job; one would think that since I was working two jobs that that would be sufficient enough for my kids and I, but unfortunately it wasn't. There were times when some of the utilities were cut off because I couldn't afford to pay the bills. Eventually I had to seek assistance from the government and get on welfare. This was one of the hardest decisions I had to make for my family. At first I didn't want to take that route because of the negative views that come with getting assistance from the government. But I had to swallow my pride because my heart was to be a better mom for my children and if needing government help was my only other option, I had to do it. I knew that it was only going to be temporary, but that didn't stop the feeling of being embarrassed when we went into the store to go grocery shopping. The thoughts of who was watching me using food stamps, and what they were saying about my kids and me was always in my mind. I tried to remind myself that getting this assistance was helping me have more money in my pocket and to be able to supply the needs that were lacking and put food on the table. But somehow I still felt like I was letting my kids down.

I had a close childhood friend tell me, "If you need to be on aid, accept it because that's what it is there for." I felt that since she had a husband and didn't need assistance from the government that she couldn't understand my situation and the feelings that I had. I was on and off of aide for five years, but the day that I was able to get off of aide for good was one of the proudest moments in my life. To me, that meant that I was able to financially hold it down for me and my kids and that the bondage of being on aide no longer held me down. While I was working, I was also pursuing my education. I went to school to become a cosmetologist. Due to life's circumstances, I only graduated from Beauty College but never received my license. Throughout the years I would attend other colleges in hopes of getting a career going, but in the end I only ended up with more diplomas. These failed plans also caused more emotional strain on me. I was still trying to figure my life out. It seemed that every time I thought I was making a positive step that would make mine and my kids' life better, it only seemed to set me back a couple of steps. I felt like I was drowning and that there wasn't going to be an end to the disappointments that were happening in my life. The disappointments caused a void in me; it caused a sadness to come over me. I was displeased with myself as a single mother and the choices I began to make started to show that.

Let's skip ahead to thirteen years later. I married my second husband and my fourth son came out of that union. I was 40 years old when I gave birth to my youngest child. When I was growing up, I always said that I wanted four kids. But just like my first marriage, this one also failed. It was my past repeating itself all over again. Now I went from being a single mother of three kids to being a single mother of four kids. I met my second husband through a friend. At this time I was in my late 30's and there was an eleven-year age difference. He also was in a different religion than what I was used to; he was Muslim. When I married him I also converted into Islam because I felt that was the best thing to do. I was following my husband because he was the head. But as the years went on I started to rebel in my marriage; I didn't want to wear my hijab because of all of the hate I was receiving. I thought the hate was towards me, but I later found out that it was towards the religion I was in. Living in Pittsburg, I felt as if I was the only African American woman in the town practicing that religion. I didn't see anyone else like me. One time I remember being in the grocery store during a holiday and the cashier was holding a conversation about the holiday. All of a sudden, the man in front of me turned around and asked me in a nasty tone if I believed in Jesus. He had the angriest look on his face. I was new to the religion and I didn't know what to say or how to respond to what was going on. After that incident I was very afraid for my life. I started to feel as if my life was in danger because of my choice in religion. This caused me to start looking over my shoulder when I was in public. I stopped wearing my hijab two years into my marriage due to the ignorant comments and the negative looks I was receiving from people. This put a strain on my marriage. My husband gave me an ultimatum, that I either started back wearing my hijab or our marriage would be over. Well, I decided that the marriage would have to be over because I was not going to continue to do something that I was not comfortable with. This marriage was an eye opening experience for me; it made me stronger and it also made me realize that not all things are as they seem. I had to learn this the hard way. I stepped into a religion head first without doing any research on it.

After my second marriage ended I spent some time dating, but I wasn't satisfied with just dating. I wanted more. I wanted to be married and I wanted to be a wife. I remember one day I was on my knees praying and crying out to God to give me a husband. About one month later I ran into an old classmate that I hadn't seen in many years. I didn't even know he was living in Pittsburg. Little did I know that he was going to be the answer to my prayers. He had come to visit the church that I was attending. During the service I noticed that he was looking at me, but I wasn't thinking anything of it until after service when he followed me outside and asked for my number and if he could call me. From that day on we started talking and getting to know each other. Shortly after that, we started dating. A year into dating we decided to get married. During the time we were dating we used to talk about how we believed that God put us together because we both were praying for a mate. We respected each other and truly loved each other. I loved my husband with all of my heart and truly felt that I had found my true love or rather my true love had found me. My husband is a preacher, so being a preacher's wife was something that I had to get used to. It was hard at first but I had to grow up and learn how to be the wife of a preacher, but there were some outside interferences that made it a struggle. These interferences caused our marriage to weaken. God was no longer in the center of our marriage and this started to pull us apart. But with me being the woman of God that I am, I was not going to let anything or anyone tear our marriage apart. With help from our Lord and Savior, we are working on strengthening our marriage.

The one important thing that I learned during my three marriages was that if God didn't send it, then it's not meant to be. God wants to give us the desires of our hearts, but if it's not something that He has for us then it's not going to work out no matter how hard we try to make it work.

The moral of my story is that sometimes we make choices that we regret; we make choices to provide for our families, even if it's a choice that we're not completely comfortable with. Now I'm a totally different woman. I am completely sold out to Christ; the darkness that I was in is no longer there. I now see the light at the end of the tunnel. I praise God with all that I have because I now know that it was Him that got me through all of my dark times. My life is centered on God. I pray more, I talk to Him more and He talks back. He told me that everything is going to be all right and that He's not done with me yet. That was the most wonderful feeling to know that God is working things out for my good. I was amazed at how He was changing my life. I now realize that putting Him first and following the path that He has laid out for me is making my life better. You may ask how am I pursuing my purpose? Well, I'm following the path that God has laid out for me; He had plans for me even before I was born. He knew that I was going to go through struggles and heartache, but He ultimately knew that when the time came for me to make a choice, either choose Him or the world and my own desires, that I was going to choose him. My purpose is to live for Jesus, to follow Him, to go where He wants me to go, to do what He wants me to do and to say what He wants me to say. I have strength now and it only comes from Him. I no longer have to worry about living my life to please people. The only person I want to please is my Heavenly Father. I no longer have to worry about the negativity from other people stealing my joy, peace and happiness. I am no longer in bondage over what others think or say about me. I just pray for them and give it to God.

I got my smile back and now it's legit. I'm still discovering my purpose and pursing it through Christ. No more tears, they have all dried up. No more brokenness, God has restored me and made me whole. No more walking in darkness, I now walk in the light of Jesus. In John 8:12 (*King James Version*) the scripture says, "Then spake Jesus again unto them, saying, I am the light of the world: he that followeth me shall not walk in darkness, but shall have the light of life."

Anita McAllister Bio:

Anita Davis McAllister is a resident of the Bay Area. She was born in Detroit, Michigan but moved to California at the age of 9. Although Anita was raised in a single parent home, her mother was very strict in the way she raised her. Her mother installed morals in her that have helped shape her into the woman she is today. Anita has instilled those same values in her kids. Anita has 4 children and 3 grandchildren and she has been married for 10 years. Anita has worked in the child care field for over 20 years as she enjoys taking care of others.

Anita feels that God has placed the gift of writing in her, and she is currently in the process of writing a book of prayers. In 2014, Anita started Spoken Word ministry, and the main focus is "Bringing people to God and saving souls". Anita also has a desire to help people. In the future, Anita inspires to start a ministry to help the homeless. Through her books, ministry group, and public speaking; Anita hopes to inspire others to take charge of their lives and follow their dreams.

"Stepping Out On Faith"

By

Keisha Frowner

Age 40

Author ~ Educator ~ Speaker ~ Mother

http://keishafrowner.wixsite.com/author

Email: klaugh983@yahoo.com

Phone :(925)238-8859

My Bishop preached two messages that inspired me, "Breaking Free from Limitations" and "Finishing Strong". After I had my children I had become complacent. I felt stuck in some ways and did not know how to get unstuck. There had to be more to life than going to work and coming home. There were some days of frustration. Raising my girls as a single parent was not easy. I knew I had to provide for my daughters and not make an excuse. I am starting to realize that God's timing is best. The things I went through were not wasted. What the devil meant for evil God turned it around for my good.

Around 2004, I started to keep a journal and write down my feelings. I was going through tough times and needed to express myself. While writing in my journal I learned a lot about myself. Each time God would reveal something new. In 2008, the church I was attending had a women's group called "The Women of Purpose". The ministry focused on women finding their purpose, along with bible study. Going to this group was like a mirror reflection at the time. The Lord was showing me the truth about myself. Soon after that there was a local author who wrote a book geared toward women. The title of the book jumped out at me because it gave me confirmation of what I was going through at that time in my life. The author put on a book-publishing workshop and I attended. The thought of me becoming an author was starting to become a reality, but there lay ahead a process. I remembered being asked at the workshop why I wanted to be an author and I stood up and said, "I want to be an inspiration to others." The workshop encouraged me to keep writing. They also had other local authors there to share their testimonies. After the workshop, I kept in contact with the author and followed her on social media. I bought her books and attended the workshops that she put on to support her because I wanted to learn more about being an author and the steps I needed to take.

About two years ago I was in Target and a woman of God came up to me and gave me an encouraging word about being around people that would embrace me. She also prayed for me. What I got from it is that I needed to be around other like-minded women that understood what I had been through. Another confirmation came at a class that I was going to at the church when a minister said the same thing as he was teaching the class. I remember asking God within myself, "Where are the people that I can relate to?" I still continued to write and journal. On New Year's Day of the next year, I wrote down becoming an author as one of my goals. Although I did not know how it would happen I stayed faithful to the process and put my trust in God. It was not easy because sometimes people can be your critics when they do not see the blessing right away. You can get caught up in how they feel about you.

I had no choice but to put my confidence in God and not man. My opportunity came on July 9, 2016, when I was a featured author in the book *Breaking through Barriers*. It all started by going to a book signing in the summer of 2015 where all I wanted to do was support someone who had written a book about relationships that were very real to me. I remember reading the book and sharing with my co-workers. After the book signing, the connection was made and my opportunity of becoming an author became a reality. The words that were spoken by two different people who encouraged me were starting to make sense, because at the time I was not thinking outside the box. I thank God for having me take a bold step of faith of sharing my testimony in a book. It truly is a blessing to work with other women who are pursuing their purpose. I had to trust the process even when I did not know when it would happen.

This process is helping me get out of my comfort zone. It is also helping me step out and be around other people. It is not meant for me to do it alone and you need others to help achieve your goals. Looking back at the process that God took me through, I helped sow into someone's vision. I believe whatever it is you want to do, help someone else get there and not think only about yourself. This is what I am learning and God is faithful. My daughters have been my inspiration. My youngest daughter told me before I became an author what the title of my book should already be. I asked her why she chose the title for me and she said because I keep going. Her words encourage me because I understand when you achieve a goal, you have to keep going and not stay stuck on the last goal that was achieved. My girls got to witness their mom step out on faith. I am setting the tone for the next generation in my family. I want to leave a legacy for my daughters.

You are never too old to do what God has called you to do. The things that I went through have helped me know what my purpose is. I want to help others, especially single parents, to let them know that they matter to God and He knows what they are going through when people do not understand their pain. Recently I talked with a single mom who has two children and is going to college. She talked about making sacrifices for her children. This encouraged me because I was able to relate and also encourage her to pursue what it is she wants to do. God has you on his mind and it is His timetable of when your dreams will come to pass, not the opinions of others.

Stepping out on faith required my participation, not sitting on the sidelines waiting for something to come to me. I have to put in the work to make it a reality. My book will be coming out soon. I discovered that writing is one of my passions. One thing in this journey is that there will be distractions along the way when pursuing purpose, which is why I have to stay focused. I'm going after everything God has for me in this season and this is just the beginning.

Keisha Frowner Bio:

Keisha Frowner was born in Los Angeles, CA and raised in Oakland, CA. Keisha is also an author, educator, and inspiring speaker. Growing up in Oakland, she was exposed to many things, such as drug and gang activity within her neighborhood. Staying active in church and playing basketball helped Keisha stay focused. At a young age she learned the importance of having a good work ethic. Keisha graduated from Fremont High School in Oakland, CA and went on to attend a community college. After completing her first year of college, Keisha found out that she was pregnant and was forced to leave school to take care of her child. After having both of her daughters and becoming a single mother, Keisha went back to school and received her A.A. degree at Diablo Valley College. Even though she faced adversity being a single mother of two beautiful daughters, she never gave up, despite her circumstances. She may have endured domestic violence and living in transitional housing, but Keisha never allowed anything to stop her. Keisha pushed through all setbacks in life. She was able to persevere and create a better life for her and her daughters. She always had a dream of becoming an author and in July 2016 that dream came a reality. She is a featured author in *Breaking through Barriers Volume* 2 and she was a speaker at the book launch. Keisha is currently working on her 1st solo book set to release late 2017. Through her sharing of her testimony, her books, and future speaking, Keisha wants to inspire others to never let go of their dreams and to finish what they start. Keisha credits her two beautiful daughters, Lorenna and Charlene, for being her motivation to persevere in life.

Surviving Even Though the Odds are Against Me

By

Sherron Meadows

Age 45

Author ~ Real Estate Sales Associate for Kiper Homes

quinesileo@yahoo.com

Oakley, CA

I have many unsaid stories that have happened to me in my lifetime. I believe that today I will be set free as I unleash and speak out against those things which have held me back and kept me from discovering and pursuing my true purpose in life. I will be launched into a new realm of discovering who I am. I have been held back by shame, fear, guilt and regret, to name a few. Finding out who you want to become and what you want to do in your life can be a challenge. Often times we have big dreams and hopes for our future, but often hit a roadblock and life suddenly stops. It can be caused from bad decisions we have made in our lives, medical reasons, financial reasons, pain inflicted on us as a children, allowing unnecessary events to take place in our lives as an adult, and unexpected life changing events.

I have faced many challenges in my life, but no matter what struggles came my way I decided to keep moving forward and to never look back, no matter what the cost. I have come to a point in my life where regret is no longer an option. I can only move forward from where I am today in my life and expect the best.

As a young girl I wanted to be a nurse and I told myself that when I finished high school I would go right to college and pursue my dreams. I wanted to help others by nursing them back to good health. I was good at consoling others when life was not going good, encouraging them to do better in life, no matter what difficulties they faced, and helping them to discover their gifts and talents. I enjoyed pulling the good out of people. While I was encouraging others, I began to face my own obstacle at nineteen years old when I gave birth to my daughter. I was going to school at that time to become a Medical Receptionist. I figured it was my foot in the door. Although, I finished school I didn't get jobs working in a hospital. This was the beginning of my dreams passing me by. Life began to happen and I had more children. I later began working full-time at a job during the day and going to school full-time in the evening. As the years started passing me by, my dreams were getting further behind me. I've never regretted having my children, who I get to sit back and watch complete and pursue their dreams.

What I failed to realize in my own life was that while I was encouraging others, I needed to be encouraged myself. I didn't have a positive role model in my life to lift me up and send me in the right direction at a young age. I left home at the age of fifteen and moved in with one of my best friends and her mother. I then moved back home a couple of times, but from that moment I was basically on my own. I got a job at a local McDonalds and provided for my own needs. Although, I was away from home and on my own, I still found myself encouraging my friends to go to school and not give up on life. There was a group of us girls who all hung out and stuck together through thick and thin. It seemed that almost every friend that I encountered at a young age was growing up in, or grew up in, a household where there was some sort of an addiction and abuse. I vowed to myself to never get hooked on drugs or to become an alcoholic. I wanted my children to be able to lean on me and not on the streets. My heart's desire is to see others grow and advance in life. I believe that there is greatness in each and every one of us, and we all have a will to survive. We just need someone to pull the greatness out of us when necessary.

At a very young age I had a will to survive. I don't remember a lot of good times that happened before the age of twelve, but I am sure there had to have been some. I feel that I have blocked a lot of things from my memory. At the age of five I was kidnapped, or I guess you could say, I got in the car with a stranger. I would walk home from school every day and there was a little boy that would chase me home and would sometimes beat me up. On one particular day I didn't want him to beat me up. He had recently drug me in my nice new baby blue fur coat, so I tried to take a different way home, and got lost. I can still see his face – the man that took me that day. He reminded me a little of Abraham Lincoln. The white hair that covered his face also reminded me a little of Santa Claus. We all trust Santa as little kids. I thought I would be safe. The thought of being found in a ditch later that evening never crossed my mind. I can remember getting into his car and being found in a ditch by the police. I don't remember anything that happened after getting into his car nor in between. I only remember being found by the police and taken home to my mother.

I was molested at a young age by one of my relatives. My sisters and I would sleep on the floor at my grandmother's house and one of my uncles would come into the room at night and molest us. I could remember lying there and praying to God that he would not come to me that night. I love my sisters, but each night I would pray that it would not be my night. Sometimes I wondered if my sisters would pray that same prayer. There were times when my grandmother would sit up in the middle of the bed while my uncle was in the room. Sometimes I wondered if she sat up in the bed because she heard a noise or was she hearing our cries in the middle of the night. I didn't like going to my grandmother's house at all, but we dared not whisper what was happening to us in the midnight hour.

At the age of thirteen, I hated my life and wanted to commit suicide. I was leaving my friends behind on my thirteenth birthday and moving to a place I had never been before. We moved around a lot and on my thirteenth birthday I remember getting on a bus and leaving my only friends that I had made in a very long time. Before them, I had one friend that I had left behind in Indianapolis. I still remember her name. It was not easy for me to make friends because we moved around a lot and I was very shy. I would get teased a lot at school and people would make fun of me. I was very insecure and thought I was very ugly. The name some of my family members and the kids at school would call me was "blacky", "dark vador", and "Grace Jones". I grew up having a complex about being dark skinned and always wished I had lighter skin. The friends that I had come to make in Arizona were friends that I knew I would keep forever. They were ones who accepted me as I was, never talked about me and I was beautiful to them. I did not want to leave them, but I had to say goodbye that day. I should have been having my sweet thirteen party and celebrating with my friends, but instead this was my move from Tucson to California. We lived in a shelter for a while when we first reached California. We were living in downtown San Diego, where I never want to live nor see again. This is where I held painful memories as a teenager. I lost my innocence as a child, but I lost my virginity in San Diego where I was raped. This is something I have never shared with my mother. We then moved into our new apartment in Chula Vista. One day I was walking down our street and went through a fenced area in order to get to school. I was raped again that day by two young men who were hanging out in the park, smoking weed, and drinking. This was another story that I never shared. I felt in those times that there was something I had to have done for this to happen to me.

Shortly after that, I left San Diego and moved back to Arizona. I was fifteen and I was no longer the person I was when I left at thirteen. I was promiscuous and immediately got into a relationship with an older person that I should not have been with. This person was in a gang and was a drug dealer. I went into the relationship knowing this, but felt secure that because he was a "bad boy" he could protect me. No one would ever hurt me again. Although I loved him, I did find it within myself to leave him when I was nineteen. Our relationship was always on and off. There were many years of pain and sadness. I struggled with depression, suicidal thoughts, insecurities and much more.

Twenty years later, I married the same person I fell in love with when I was fifteen. Although, we had gone our separate ways, had children, and moved on in our lives. I knew when I met him 20 years prior that he was the wrong person for me and I knew 20 years later that he was still the wrong person for me. I was still in love with the past. My life began to take that same turn it took when I was fifteen years old. I began to have insecurities and struggled with depression, all over again. We were married in 2006 and separated in 2010. I had to pick up the pieces and start my life all over again. A wise person once told me that it doesn't take that long when you say "I do" to realize that you made a mistake. Don't stay in; get out as soon as you can. I went through all of my savings, my 401K, my credit was torn up and it only took four years to have to start over from the beginning.

I was embarrassed that I had gotten myself into a marriage that my friends had warned me about. For four years I lived with a man who was an alcoholic who would try and hide his alcohol from me. I would find beer behind the washer and dryer, in my trunk where the spare tire goes, in the closet hidden on the top shelf behind clothes, behind the outside dumpster, in the garage behind the water cooler and in many other places. I had gotten to a point in my life where I began to lose my will to live and move forward in life. I wasn't sure I could come back from this. I knew my friends had already warned me and I didn't listen. I left home one day after I had thrown things around in the garage, screamed, yelled, and cried out to God. I walked out the house with no shoes and a bottle of pills. I walked a couple of blocks down the street where there were a lot of trees and I was ready to take those pills. I had had enough of the emotional and verbal abuse, and in my eyes my life was no longer worth living. I was at my breaking point and needed a savior to guide me back. Within the darkness of the night I could hear the wind whistling and I felt the leaves of the trees rubbing up against me. I was so terrified because I could feel death near me and I was surrounded by darkness. I opened up the bottle, took the pills out and was ready for the pain to end. I yelled beyond the trees, "Why me?" At this point I wasn't just talking about the marriage; I was talking about everything. My life in general, all the way back to five years old. I then had a vision of my children without me. I could see my daughter crying, my baby boy lost without me, and my oldest boys confused and wondering why. I heard a voice within me tell me, "Don't do it. There is a reason why you are here." I immediately felt peace surrounding me. If God can use me to be a voice to others to lead them back to life, then it's what I want. I threw that bottle down and the pills that I had in my hand and I ran home, cleaned the garage, prayed and asked God for forgiveness, and carried on with my day. It was at that moment I realized that I, too, have a purpose in life. God chose me to lead my children in the right direction in life, to guide them, encourage them and help them be successful.

Today, my daughter is about to graduate from the Art Institute in San Francisco. My eldest son is about to graduate from Hunters College in New York and my eighteen-year-old just graduated from high school and entered into University of Pacific in Stockton. I don't give all the credit to myself because I did have some help from their fathers. I was a single mother all my life, even the four years I was married. I took care of home and provided for my children and myself. I've always told my children that school and college are important. I never went through life believing that my children were perfect. I know that they are capable of mistakes. I was very stern and strict with my children and for that was criticized by some family members and friends for being too hard on them. I always told my children that they would never be a statistic. Instead, they would be an asset to this world, and their name would be remembered. I always told them that they could always come back from their mistakes, to always own up to their mistakes, and never make excuses in their life. I told them they were always to respect their elders and never disrespect their mother, who was me.

I am a firm believer that you don't do well in life if you dishonor your mother and father and if you want something in your life then you have to go out there and get it. When I had my daughter at nineteen years old, I was on welfare, food stamps and Section 8. I worked through temporary services for a little while. I would get up at 4:00 in the morning, get my daughter dressed, and push her stroller to daycare if I did not have the money to get on the bus. I would then take the bus to the trolley, if I had the money to board the bus. I would take the trolley to downtown San Diego or wherever it was I had my temporary assignment. I would then get off the trolley and walk to the place of business, if it was in walking distance and if I didn't have the money to board the bus. As a single mother

I had to find programs that would help me and would allow me to step up to the next level. There are many programs out there that will help and be your stepping stone. I don't believe these programs should be geared towards us getting on them and staying there. I got my first apartment at 20 years old and worked at a toy store. I started off as seasonal help and by February I was made assistant manager. Before I became assistant manager, I worked part-time with the toy store and part-time at a bank. I do not have the tolerance for people that say that they can't find a job. There was a time in my life when I worked for two staffing agencies and tutored children part-time during the week. As a parent and an individual you have to do what is necessary to take care of your family and yourself. There were many days I was tired and at one point worked 21 days straight without a day off, eight plus hours a day. I didn't complain of being tired, I did what was necessary to take care of my children and my household. If my child was sick and I was up all night, I still had to get up and go to work. If my car broke down or I didn't have a car then I would find alternate transportation or walk.

I believe that my purpose in life is to help other young women and girls that were in my situation to find a solution. I could have stayed in that relationship where I was being emotionally and verbally abused, but I chose to take a different route. I was embarrassed to share what I was really going through until I figured out that I was never alone and I told myself that I had been a fighter all my life. I can't give up when the road gets bumpy. I want to make a difference for others and help them find a better solution. If we are in a bad situation or we do not like what we are seeing in our lives, then we are the only ones that can change our situations. I don't believe that God intended for us to stay in abusive situations and live our lives less than we need to. My dreams of helping people as a nurse may or may not be in the future for me, but I know that within me I have the nature to help others. Recently there was a situation when my son was sick and in the emergency room. There was a young lady that had a black eye and her boyfriend had been abusing her. I went to the restroom and she, too, was waiting for the restroom. She began to talk to me and share a little bit of her story and at that moment I began to speak life and purpose into her. Her eyes lit up as tears streamed down her face. She said to me, "I grew up in an abusive household and I never realized that I could have something different in life until now." That was the moment I discovered my purpose in life. I may not be a nurse with a degree and working in the hospital, but with my mouth I will encourage, nurture, influence, build up, and do whatever is necessary to build up every person's self-esteem and willingness to survive, be prosperous, not give up on themselves and strive to be happy. I believe it is a gift that

God gave me and I will use it to help others find their true purpose.

I have made it through many trials and tribulations in my lifetime, even though surviving when the odds were against me seemed unreachable. August 2017, I will be coming out with a book called *Secrets between Sisters.* I believe my secrets will change the course of many young girls' and women's lives. We no longer have to be bound by what was inflicted on us by others, nor do we have to be ashamed of decisions we made that caused us pain. We can change lives together by opening our mouths and speaking out. We will survive together.

Sherron Meadows Bio:

Sherron Meadows is a single mother of four. Her oldest is 25 and her youngest is nine. She is the second youngest of three brothers and two sisters and was born in Illinois. Sherron has always been a hard worker and a strong believer that hard work pays off and everything obtained in your life comes at a price. She started her first job at thirteen, selling candy bars door to door and has been working full-time since the age of nineteen. She became a mother at the age of nineteen. She was raised in a single parent home where there was little affection or love shown and her mother struggled with an alcohol addiction. From the struggles she faced with her upbringing, she vowed that she would show her children what love looked like and teach them about unconditional love. At the age of 30, she had a nervous breakdown and a stroke. Sherron passionately believes that your circumstance does not have to dictate your outcome. If you don't like what you see in your life than you have to be willing to do something different to get better results. Sherron has always wanted to be a nurse, but has faced many challenges in life being a single mom. She believes that even though she is not a nurse, she can still nurse people back to good health through conversation, by lifting them up with encouraging words, and the reading of her books. She firmly believes that no matter what people do to you, you are still able to love them. Her mission is to inspire and encourage single mothers and young women to not give up on their journey in life and their dreams. Believing that everyone has a purpose in life, she wants to help others reach their goals. Sherron's future goals include starting a non-profit organization for abused women and children by providing them with a safe place to call home, as well as, accomplishing her goal of becoming a motivational speaker for women.

"I'm Coming Out"

By

Monique Mccoy

Age: 32

Author ~ Writer ~ Motivational Speaker

Email: itzmorning007@gmail.com

Follow me on Facebook @ Monique Mccoy

Instagram @moeministry

I was at a music celebration and a music critic said, "Donald Matthews is going to be a great writer some day when he suffers more." And I said to myself, what does that mean? Now I know what it means.

If you know where this line comes from, then you, my friend, are all right with me! Yes, this is a line from my favorite movie, *The Five Heartbeats*. I identify with "Duck" every time I watch that scene. Now here I am after a little suffering on this journey, sharing my story with you!

I don't belong here! This is what I've said to myself for the last ten years. How did I go from an ambitious adolescent to living idly in a 6 x 8 foot cell? I'm not sure that I really know how I got to this point. My mom's golden rule was to go to school, get good grades and get a job; and maybe college, as long as it didn't interfere with your job. I had done all three and dabbled in a few college courses. For a long time I never understood why she was so militant about working. Besides, it wasn't like she came from a poor home. My grandmother was a schoolteacher and my grandfather was a MUNI Supervisor, and they both were prominent figures in the community. I'd seen pictures of their yearly vacations to Disneyland and Santa Cruz. She and my uncles even grew up in a house on Palou Street, with stairs and a basement (I always wanted to live in a house!). My mother, however, found herself on the other side of town on Palou Ave. Things were a little different over there. Let's just say, we had a lot of traffic in and out of our house. We had stairs only because it was a three-story building. She worked so hard you'd think she was a single mom! She always put work before anything else, like that was the only thing guaranteed in life. By the time I was twelve years old, I had my first job through YCD (Young Community Developers), a non-profit organization in San Francisco, California. I had the opportunity to pick up trash on the weekends; the same trash that me and my knucklehead friends had distributed over time. It was cool making my own change.

Growing up in San Francisco's Hunter's Point projects, you grow up really fast. Either by the influences that surround you, or because you have no choice but to put on two pair of socks and wear someone else's shoes. For me it was both. As my mom worked retail jobs with hours that didn't correlate with "Back to School Night", my sisters and I got in where we fit in. I was the middle child, but when my older sister left home at seventeen I found myself wearing my mom's 6 ½ size shoes. I was cooking, cleaning, and walking my little sister and me to the bus stop every day. My stepfather was there, but at the same time he wasn't.

I keep a picture pinned up of my three favorite men: my husband and two sons. They keep me going. My boys are much taller now. I swear my sons' eyes look like they are looking right at me. They remind me of what life is like on the outside; natural sunlight, fresh air, and so many opportunities. There was a time when I had it all figured out. According to my journal, I should have been a well-known rapper by now. I never had a plan B. I never wanted to be a doctor or a lawyer. I never wanted to go to college, unless it was for music, public speaking or some form of art. No plan B, just a dope rapper and producer. I found out later that that opportunity wasn't just going to land in my lap. You have to work for what you want. You have to consistently work on your craft. That's where I failed, but I knew how to keep a job, if nothing else. The rap dream vanished over time, but my love for writing never left. In fact, I've written quite of few stories since I've been locked up. Writing is the only way I've ever known how to truly express myself. I wrote the story about my relationship with my father. How an addict, sold out for Jesus, taught his daughter about the bible. My father said he cried like a baby the night he received my package in the mail. He couldn't even sleep. I think it gave him closure. I had finally forgiven him for popping in and out of my life. I also wrote "Strawberry Sundae", a short story about my shopping excursions with my grandmother and how McDonald's ice cream sundaes bonded us in the sweetest way, even after her death. Somehow I feel like she's proud of me, even though I'm not exactly where I want to be.

I have come a long way though. Those influences growing up in San Francisco stuck with me for a long time. Even after moving out of the hood at fourteen years old. You know the saying, "You can take the girl out of the hood but you can't take the hood out of the girl." I started smoking at a young age. It started off with Beedies (Remember those?). You could buy a 24 pack of those Indian cancer sticks for a couple bucks. And the liquor store clerk never asked for ID. I remember I got suspended in middle school after the teacher found a pack in my backpack. Weed, among other things, were heavily exchanged up and down 3rd street like dollars and cents. I'd learned how to negotiate two (10 sacks) for 15 (dollars) early on. There I was in the 7th grade walking down the strip. There was a certain type of eye contact you made to let people know you were looking for weed. I could roll blunts better than the guys my step dad hung out with. My older sister was even surprised. She had no clue that I smoked. It was like an art every time I rolled a blunt. I was precise with each tuck and twist, sealing it with a little saliva and flame from someone's lighter from the night before. Believe it or not, I got heavily involved with weed and alcohol when we moved to the suburbs. They say you haven't really been high until you've smoked with the "white boys". They introduced me to pipes and bongs. It was a whole new world, coming from zigzags and blunts. As years passed by it was my go to, first thing in the morning and the last thing at night. I even began smoking on my way to work, on my breaks, and lunches too! Blunts and Black and Mild's (Remember those?) was all I knew. I was like a walking zombie, but never lazy; I always had a job. I guess that's how I justified my addiction. Every now and then I'd end up with a laced blunt. I could tell because my lip would get numb, but that didn't stop me. Sometimes I swore I heard my brain sizzling. It was crazy, but it was like I couldn't function without it.

My creativity was insane. I had this red light in my room and I'd turn it on, play an instrumental, and either write a dope flow or write poems in my journal. I've been a deep thinker ever since I was a kid. Getting high took me into the depths of my thoughts. I even found myself reading the Bible when I was high. As a kid, I used to think so much about life that I thought something was wrong with me. I'd be like, "Go play, why are you thinking about God and death and the meaning of life, go play with some dolls or something!" But that's just the way I was wired: inquisitive, passionate and discerning! It can be overwhelming sometimes, but I truly believe it's a gift from God. All I ever knew was to grab a pen and transfer my thoughts on to paper.

My relationship with weed started to dissipate after my grandmother died from cancer. I got this weird feeling, like I needed to get my life together. Like an epiphany. That was right around the time my friend's younger sister told me I looked old. My friend and I had smoked and were hanging out around the house and out of nowhere her eleven-year-old sister looked at me with the concern of a grandmother and said, "You look old!" She might as well have said I looked like sh*t. I played it cool, but transitioned to the bathroom and for the first time I saw how tired I looked. That weed, drank, and my overall lifestyle were doing a number on me. I was only 20 years old.

Another thing that I was dealing with was depression. But like many other African Americans in the black community, I've never felt comfortable talking about it. Talking to a therapist was out of the question, except for this one time when I learned I could get six to eight weeks away from a job I hated if I acted depressed. The word on the street was, if they ask if you're suicidal you just say yes! According to my journal I should have been an actress by now, too. I had my debut in the psychiatrist's office. Most of what I said was exaggerated, but deep down inside there was some truth. I'd be lying if I said I wasn't tempted to open up, but my pride held me hostage. That's exactly what pride does! After two sessions and one group meeting, I threw away those unopened pills and fell off the face of the earth. If you ask anyone that suffers from depression they will testify that it comes when it wants to. Things can be going great and then, boom! This big dark cloud decides to take a rest stop (not pit stop) over your head.

It follows you everywhere you go. It's like a bully, that never really tells you why it's bothering you, just that it will be here and will leave when it feels like it. It doesn't matter how much money you have or your social status, it doesn't discriminate. Some of our greatest influencers suffer from this mental illness. When I heard that Robin Williams had taken his own life due to depression, my heart sank in my chest. This man released the weight of the world off many shoulders whenever he opened his mouth. Oh yeah, and there's no look to it. You'd be surprised how many people you know personally who suffer from depression, including yourself.

They say time flies when you're having fun. Well, time also flies when you're daydreaming and stuck in a place where you have settled. I feel like I have settled here. I've mastered daydreaming ever since I was a kid. I've seen myself at the BET Awards saying, "First I'd like to give honor to God..." I've seen myself dressed in a tailored suit, having lunch with a client at twelve noon. I've even seen myself on a vacation drinking lemonade in the shade. But, here I am in this box. Others here seem like they have dreams, too. This one lady loves arts and crafts and another lady loves to write just like me. She even published a children's book about her son called *Spaghetti Sam*. I can see the years wearing on them. So much locked up potential. I've been told over the years that I don't belong here. "Monique, I can't picture you here forever, you have so much potential." My mom even called the other day and said that my stories are getting around and encouraging so many people. Deep down inside I know it! But sometimes I feel like I'm institutionalized. That's a term used to describe someone who keeps going in and out of the prison system. No matter how many times they get out, even with support and resources provided, they find a way to get caught up again. I've been in and out of a few different systems, but this last one I've called home for about five years now. Your only identity is the 7-digit number that records everything you touch. But like always, writing has helped me get through many dark days, literally (there is no sunshine in here).

Speaking of dark days. Writer's block had come through like a tornado and wiped out every thought of inspiration. For years I swore it was because I wasn't getting high anymore, but I knew I was a creative being far before my "how high" days. I had relied on the weed too much. So much that I thought I was nothing without it. I felt like a superhero that had lost her powers. But I hadn't lost my powers at all. I was changing and my views of the world were changing. God was calling me to live for Him. That meant I had to die to my old ways and it definitely didn't happen overnight. The content that I wrote about in the past was not pleasing to God. I was a new creation in Christ (2 Corinthians 5:17). See, when you are going through withdrawal from a dark world full of sin, you will feel all kinds of ways. Picture a spiritual exorcism: sweating, screaming, foaming at the mouth, confusion and resistance. But in the end you are free! Free to be who you were called to be all along.

After I had received Christ as my Lord and Savior, I knew I had a greater purpose. But that was it. Knowing and doing are two different things. I didn't know exactly where I belonged. I knew it had something to do with writing or speaking, but I was stuck. So I became comfortable with just existing. I wasn't being truly who God had called me to be. And deep down inside I was empty. I spent years in a spiritual wilderness. I was blending in with the crowd, going from job to job just to seek higher pay. I was giving my all to help the CEO fulfill his dreams. I was still writing sporadically, but I didn't know how to express myself anymore. I watched so many people walk in their purpose and live their dreams. How could I walk around with so much greatness inside of me and not share it with the world? Like a butterfly stuck in a cocoon. People would ask me what I did for a living and I wouldn't tell them I was a writer or that I loved music. I would just tell them where I worked at the time. Time was moving right before my eyes and when I finally came to my senses I was in my 30's and still here in this box.

Now I know I have shared a lot with you. But I know you really want to know how I got myself locked up. What happened?

It's only right that I finally tell you. But before I do, can I ask you a couple of questions? Have you ever wanted something so badly, but at the same time felt so afraid of having it? Sounds crazy, right? Have you ever been afraid of the sacrifices that it requires?

I had followed my mom's golden rule. But I lost my individuality along the way. No friends, I'm not in jail. I may have made some mistakes in my life, but my mom taught me better than that! But what makes a dead-end job any different? I've worked at call centers all my life and I've sat amongst some of the most brilliant human beings. I've seen some of the greatest talent sit and rot right before my eyes. I work for a great company and make good money. But, there is more to life than settling for a paycheck at the cost of our destiny. Someone once told me that in order to get to the next level in your life you have to get uncomfortable. I've been beyond uncomfortable lately. But, the beautiful thing about life is that every morning that God allows you to rise, no matter where you are in life, He gives you another chance to start over. You have to use the lessons from yesterday as a compass for the days ahead. I read an interesting article that really spoke to me called, "5 steps to turn your passion into your profession" by Steve Knox. Here is an excerpt from the article:

"Passion is a funny thing. It keeps you up at night and sparks something deep inside you. It inspires you to try and change the world, or at least make your little corner a bit better. Your frustrations often reveal your passions. So many people say it would be great if they could just quit their day job and pursue their passion full time to start a business or write a book or launch a blog. But that's all it is, talk. To those people, I say: Stop talking about it and do something. Turn your passion into your profession."

So although I may be in this box a little while longer. This box no longer defines me. This book is evidence of that. Don't worry mom, I'm not going to just quit my job. I know I have to start somewhere. But you have to trust me on this one. I know who I am now and where I belong.

My name is Monique and I am a writer and motivational speaker and I'm coming out!

Steve Knox, Steve "5 Steps to Turn Your Passion into Your Profession"

(August 23, 2016, www.success.com)

Monique McCoy Bio:

Born and raised in the heart of San Francisco's Hunter's Point projects, Monique McCoy knows first-hand how violence, addiction, and low self-esteem can affect generations in the community. Her love for writing surfaced at a young age, where she began to transfer her thoughts onto paper through song, poetry and storytelling. Monique's passion for the well being of others is evident in her blog titled "Itz Morning", where she provides thought-provoking perspectives about everyday life. Her mission is to encourage self-love and self-development through motivational speaking. Monique is a member of Toastmasters international, an Ambassador for her local Chamber of Commerce, and sits on the committee for the Chamber's "Empowering Ladies in Leadership" organization. She resides in Antioch, California with her husband and two sons.

Life Path

By

Danae Braggs

Age 37

Real Estate Agent ~Author ~ Entrepreneur ~ Speaker

and all around Superwoman

Pittsburg, CA Native

Business Cell: 925-481-6058

Looking back over the past 24 years, she unwillingly replays scenes in her head of time after time when her good intentions were misunderstood and awesome opportunities were passed over due to not only her own insecurities, but the insecurities topped with the selfish wants and needs of others.

The continuous realization that the selfishness of others was a determining factor in most of the life changing decisions that were made either for her, or by her, haunt her to this day. Looking back, her life path at this point is riddled with happy moments clouded by sad shadows and bad hair days.

She often wonders what would have been different if she had made a different choice at any of the crossroads in her past. What, if anything, could be different about now? The fond awareness of her life path philosophy and her newfound eagerness to share it with those she encounters are both signs that all the choices made – bad or good – led right up to this very moment. *"All things work together for good"*. So goodbye, shoulda, woulda, coulda... Hello, woman on a mission.

This woman fueled by misunderstandings and low expectations is on a mission to recapture those missed opportunities and make up for lost time. She's determined to not be labeled with any demeaning statistic and to help others avoid it as well. She fully embraces and shares what she calls the life path.

What, exactly, is this life path? The definition is pretty simple...

The life path is the road map, so to speak, marked with the results of every decision made by you, on your behalf, or decisions made by someone else in their life that directly affected you. It essentially connects every moment of your life with every decision made, ultimately leading you to the time and space that you are in right now. For example: You made the decision to pick up this book and your thought process may be affected by what you read in it. The decision to read this book can potentially affect every aspect of your life going forward. The life path philosophy suggests that everything that happens in one moment makes you who and what you are in the next moment and the cycle continues until your last breath. Powerful, right?

Reflecting on how you got where you are can be painful and can bring up a lot of different emotions. You have to keep in mind that without the bad you wouldn't know how good the good is. It's a necessary process for growth.

So let me introduce you to her... Her name is Danae, pronounced like Renee. She is me. I am her. To know where you're going, you have to realize and accept where you've been. Welcome to your life path.

Danae Braggs Bio:

A Pittsburg, CA native, Danae Braggs is an all-around SUPER WOMAN. Becoming a mother at 16, she had every reason to also become a statistic. She never did. She soared above the odds and surpassed a lot of lack luster expectations. Today she is a successful entrepreneur, real estate agent, and author; just to name a few of her many accomplishments. Her philanthropic endeavors almost always promote her beloved city, Pittsburg. She is also the secretary of Branches of Community Services, a local non-profit focused on giving back to our youth and our community. She has been quoted as saying "I'm from here from here..." An advocate for children, housing rights, self-sufficiency and more, Danae shows and proves that she is the epitome of the term SUPER WOMAN.

Breaking Through

The Impossible

Lessons Turned Into Blessings

By

Eshe' Satcher

Author ~ Lead Coordinator ~ Educator ~ Mother

Age 33

Pittsburg, CA

As a child, I was taught not to talk to other people about what happened in my household. As I am typing this, I am wondering why a parent would tell their children that; unless they have something to hide. I lived in several areas around Pittsburg, California, such as, West Pittsburg (Bay Point) and Antioch. What shaped me into the person that I am today were my experiences when I lived in Pittsburg, near the high school. I feel like my story starts with my parent's story. I am choosing not to talk about my experiences in relationships with men, in detail. I will save that for another book.

My mother was raised in Fresno and Pittsburg and my father was raised in Alabama. My father was drafted into the Air Force at the age of eighteen and was well traveled. He even went to Africa. He was shot in the leg during the Vietnam War and was honorably discharged. He received his Bachelor's degree in Political Science from Fresno State University. My mother and father met in Fresno during that time. Most of my mother's side of the family is located in Pittsburg and Fresno. My mom did not have a relationship with a lot of her family members, which caused us to not know a lot of them until we were older. My mother was raised by her grandmother. Her mother was not able to support her because she started having children at a very young age and she was a diabetic. I believe my grandmother was about fourteen years old when she started having children. When my great grandmother passed away, my mother was in labor. When I was born, my father named me Eshe'. All of my siblings' first or middle names have a meaning. As I was growing up, my dad always told me that Eshe' meant "life" in Swahili. In total, my parents had four children, two boys and two girls. My parents decided to move back to Pittsburg to be closer to my mom's family. My parents had a seven year age difference and were together for over 20 years, but they never were married.

My father made us understand the importance of education and family. He was big on respecting our elders and staying out of adult conversations. We used to get spankings when we would get in trouble. Also, he instilled this in everyone that was in his presence. I miss him calling me on my birthdays to sing me happy birthday. Also, I miss him cooking soul food or gumbo around the holidays. He would always tell me how beautiful I was and I loved spending time with him. When we would ask my dad what he wanted for his birthday, he would say that he just enjoyed being alive and spending time with us. He was never materialistic. My dad was very spiritual and would tell us the stories that were in the Bible. I remember riding around the neighborhood and he would wave at everyone he saw. I would ask him if he knew the person and he would say he didn't.

To add, my father felt strongly about receiving a good education because he grew up in Alabama during the Civil

Rights Era. My father and his twin brother were the first black students to attend a school that was once segregated. He used to tell us how the white students would throw rocks and spit on them. He grew up on a farm and always told us how he had to walk a mile to school. We could never tell our father that we were bored. If we did, he would tell us to go and read a book. I remember we had the Encyclopedia Britannica A - Z. He would quiz us and our other families out of nowhere, "What is 5x5?" He would say, "You should be able to say the answer without any hesitation." My father had a great sense of humor and was very proud of all of his children's accomplishments. For example, if I asked my dad where my brother was he would say, "In his skin, when he jumps out, you jump in." He encouraged a lot of my cousins to attend college and he would give all of us money for receiving good grades. He did not like it when we said we "can't" do something.

I don't remember my parents working, but I was told that my father was a teacher. I remember our water was cut off and social workers came to our school to ask us questions, but we knew not to say anything. My father was very resourceful; he knew how to cut the water back on and would run a cable to our neighbor's house when we didn't have power. We grew up in a low income household (welfare and food stamps), and didn't always have food in our refrigerator, but we had the nicest clothes. Does that make sense? My mother received county assistance and had Section 8. Both of my parents indulged in drugs and alcohol, so they had to find a way to support us and to support their habit. I remember my mother and father going to stores, stealing clothes, and selling them. They even used to take us with them, as a decoy, and at times had us taking stolen items out of the stores. My sister and I were arrested when we were children when my father was caught stealing. We would go to the toy store in the mall with a garbage bag and steal toys around Christmas. My parent used to stay up all night arguing. I remember hearing my sister always begging them to be quiet because we had school in the morning. Also, I remember the times when we didn't have food, we had to wash our clothes in the bathtub, and we had to wash our faces with socks. Hard times!

My family moved to Pittsburg when I was in the 5th grade. We moved from a four-bedroom, 3 bathroom home to a 2 bedroom, 1 bathroom home. My parents had their own room and all of us shared a room. I can remember, very clearly, the first day I went to school. It was a total culture shock because there were a lot more black students than there were in the school I attended previously. I remember checking in at the school's office and one of the students taking me to the classroom. When I entered the classroom, the teacher introduced me and slaughtered my name, of course. I use to get teased a lot by the male students about my name and the way I would dress. This is funny because many of the male students tried to talk to me when I went to junior high school (laughs). I used to love when my cousins would come over and visit. We were all raised more as sisters and brothers. My parents would allow us to have parties, drink alcohol, smoke marijuana, and have too much freedom. My father just wanted to always know where we were, but did not really tell us not to use drugs or alcohol. To think about it, how could my parent tell us not to use and they would do drugs in front of us?

When I was younger, I can remember my mother and father being in and out of jail. Unfortunately, my older brother ended up in the same situation. We were lucky to have the support of our other family members during the times when our parents were incarcerated or we would have ended up in foster care, a group home, or somewhere worse. At several points in my life I can remember our doors being kicked in by the police and both of my parents being in jail at the same time. When we lived in Pittsburg, this occurred. My older brother, who was only fifteen years old, took on the responsibly of being our parent in their absence. It was strange because it seemed that we were doing better for ourselves compared to when our parents were there. My brother made sure that all of the bills were paid and that we were clothed and fed. He even started selling marijuana and that is when all of us started really smoking. There used to be a lot of people at, and around, our house all the time. I am so thankful that I was never molested or raped.

When my mother was released from prison, I noticed a change in her personality. I found out that my mother was diagnosed with having a mental illness. I believe my mother was having mental issues before she went to jail based off of some of the stories my siblings used to tell me. When I was baby, I was told that my mother busted out all of the windows in our house. I remember one night she went around the house and put crosses on all of the doors. My mother, and other family members, have lived with me throughout my life, but it was very challenging to live with a person that has a mental illness. She would have outburst of laughing and would say the most hurtful things. I will always be there for her, but I don't feel like I have a relationship with my mother. I say this because I don't feel comfortable talking to her about any of my problems nor does she seem to care. I always had a closer relationship with my father, but I still respect my mother. When both of my parents were released from custody, their relationship with each other, and with us, changed. I can say that we did not respect our parents the same. My older brother started getting involved with harder drugs. I remember my father and brother got into an argument and my brother shot my dad in the stomach with a .25. I was pleading with him not to do it and I was next to my dad when it happened. When my brother shot the gun, he ran, and I saw my father fall. The ambulance came to pick my father up, immediately, and my brother was later taken to jail. My father did not want to press charges, but the district attorney did, so my brother ended up going to jail.

Shortly after these incidents, I was told that my mother stopped paying the rent so all of us had to be separated and live at other people's houses. I was about thirteen years old around this time. My older sister had already had a baby at sixteen, and I felt so alone. By the time I was fourteen, I found out that I was pregnant. My cousin told me that she wanted to see if she was pregnant, so we both took a test at the local clinic. That is when I found out that I was pregnant, but I did not plan on keeping the baby. Several months had passed by and I had to move from where I was staying. I moved to my grandmother's house and tried to hide that I was pregnant. That didn't work out too well because by that time I was five months pregnant. My grandmother refused to allow me to have an abortion. What is uncanny is that my grandmother passed away a few months after I had my son. My grandmother was having a lot of health issues due to her diabetes and had been on dialysis for several years. One night she made us all a huge meal, which was odd because she did not cook a lot. The next morning, my cousin and I realized that she had not awakened. She used to be the first person awake in the house. My grandmother had passed away in her sleep. After my grandmother passed, my aunt allowed me to move with her and assisted me throughout, and after, my pregnancy.

I was able to support my son by having various jobs and moved into my own apartment when I was eighteen. My father and mother helped me raise my son as I got older, but I was still his main caregiver. According to the county, I made too much money for me to receive cash aid, but I was allotted food stamps. My brother was getting in trouble where he was staying so I ended up getting custody of my seventeen-year-old brother. My brother was never home and would travel out of state without any communication. He would always be in the streets or in "traffic". When my brother was eighteen, we moved to Pittsburg and I became worried about his lifestyle. This was in 2003. I had a conversation with him and we talked about how he needed to change his life. He had been recently arrested for having a gun and was out on bail. A couple of weeks later, I saw my brother at the gas station. I was on my way to the mall in Concord with my cousins. I remember my brother saying that I was trying to be like him by being in traffic. I did not think that would be the last conversation that I would have with my brother.

A few minutes later he was shot and soon after, passed away. This was one of the most difficult times in my life. When I heard that he passed, I felt my heart drop into my stomach. I heard a lot of negative things about why my brother was shot, but I refuse to accept the reasons for why he was murdered. Losing my brother was one of the hardest times of my life and what made it worse was that someone we grew up with was accused of his death. I forgave him, for myself, but I still deal with mourning my brother every day. I understand that "living that street life" leads to jail or death. Another challenge was that he did not have any life insurance, so we had to raise money to give him a proper burial during the time when we were supposed to be mourning. I can honestly say that his death affected a lot of people and I thank the community for financially assisting us to have his funeral. In that week period of trying to coordinate my brother's funeral and raise money, my older brother was shot in Oakland. So we had to deal with the death of my little brother and visiting my older brother in the Intensive Care Unit at the same time. He survived, but that was a very stressful time for my family.

My father passed away in 2009, at the age of 59, from prostate cancer. Seeing my father deteriorate from this disease was very challenging. He never told us how serious his condition was. I remember when he told me that his Prostate Specific Antigen (PSA) levels in his blood were high.

He was taking some type of trial medication for a few years. I knew it was serious when he told me that it had spread to his bones. The last year was extremely hard for him because he started to experience losing his balance, a loss of appetite, and hearing loss. This caused him to not be able to walk and take care of himself. He noticed that there was blood in his urine so his doctor gave him a catheter. I noticed that his appetite was decreasing, too. He was in the bed for several weeks and did not want us to take him to the hospital. His twin brother came to visit him and called the ambulance to make him go to the hospital. We had been in contact with his siblings about his health. The doctors told us that there was nothing that they could do and my father appointed me to make decisions for him during that process. I was advised that the best option for him was to go on hospice care. My father was having problems talking and swallowing food, so that slowly started to affect his health too.

A few weeks later he went to a nursing home and a couple of months later he passed away. It was hard to see my father lifeless, after he passed away. I wish I was there to hold his hand, at least. However, I was happy that my father did not have to suffer anymore. I am at peace because I was able to express everything that I needed to express to him before he passed. It was a very challenging time because my father did not have life insurance, either. My sister and I had to contact family members to assist us with his funeral costs. Also, we had to make the funeral arrangements and clean his house without the help of my mother. I miss my father every day. He loved old school music, cooking, spending time with family, reading, and fishing. I did not understand a lot of the lessons my father was trying to teach me until I became a parent and an adult. As a child, I don't remember my parents really telling us they loved us, but they tried to show it through their actions. They seemed to express their emotions more as we got older. It was very hard to lose my father because he was one of the people that kept our family together. He was buried in the veteran's cemetery a few cities over.

I can honestly say that I have been through a lot of trials and tribulations, but I refused and still refuse to give up on my goals and dreams. I appreciate the life lessons my parents taught us. I had been on welfare and was able to work my way off of receiving government assistance when I was 23 years old. My parents taught us several good and bad lessons. I have learned a lot from their mistakes and learned what not to do to, or around, my son. I was able to break through the impossible through my faith and the support of some of my family members while I attended college. I have been able to graduate college, keep a consistent job, and see my son graduate from high school. I love the job that I work at because I am working in the community that I grew up in and I feel that I am truly making a difference in a lot of people's lives. My story has just begun! I am starting to learn to change my mindset to being more positive. Since I have done this, I have been having more positive outcomes and notice that I have not been so stressed out. The moral of the story is that your past makes you who you are: Learn from your past and never give up on yourself!

This is dedicated to my father, Harry Satcher, and my younger brother, Aaron Satcher. I love you both with all of my heart.

Eshe' Satcher Bio:

Eshe' Satcher was born and raised in Pittsburg, California. She has two older siblings. She is a mother of an upstanding eighteen-year-old son who recently graduated from high school. She currently works full time as a lead supervisor for a non-profit agency that provides after school program services/events in the community of Pittsburg. Eshe' experienced a very challenging childhood, dealing with many things such as drug and alcohol addictions in the home, parents' incarceration, homelessness, as well as, her mother being diagnosed with having a mental illness and other medical issues. Eshe' became a single mother at the tender age of fifteen. She has experienced her share of tumultuous relationships and has learned a great deal of wisdom from these experiences. As a young adult, she took on the responsibly of providing a home for her younger brother. He was murdered a couple years later, at the age of eighteen. Later in her life, her father passed away from prostate cancer at the age of 59 years old. Her father, no matter what the circumstances, always stressed the importance of receiving an education and being independent. Becoming a teen mother and dealing with so much adversity in her childhood, never stopped Eshe' from being independent and it also empowered her to want more in life. She has shown her resiliency and perseverance by not allowing the challenges in life stop her from meeting her goals. Through all of her hardships, she was able to graduate high school and college. Eshe' has an Associate of Art degree in Liberal Arts and an Associate of Art degree in Business Administration. Her passion is to assist others that may be experiencing hardships in their lives and to provide them with resources to help them become successful. She is currently attending a university to receive her Bachelor of Art degree in Business with a certificate in Human Resources. Her plan is to continue to work in the education sector and to continue to be a lifelong learner. Eshe's hope is that sharing her story will help to inspire and empower others to see that anything is possible.

Spiritual Warfare

By

Andrea Taylor

Age 39

**Certified Christian Life Coach ~ Certified Career Coach ~
CEO/ Founder PYP ~ Speaker ~ Author**

Email: PYPat31@gmail.com

Website www.presentyourselfproper.com

Business (925) 207-3415

Pittsburg, CA

"Children are a gift from the Lord they are a reward from him." (*King James Version*, Psalm 127:3). I think we can all agree that one of the greatest gifts from God is to bear and raise children. It is truly a blessing. It's even more rewarding for us moms because we get to bond with our unborn babies while they're growing inside of us. The love and the bond that are established between a mother and her unborn child are uncanny. I have a number of amazing experiences that I enjoyed during my pregnancies with my three sons, but I also experienced very scary and uncertain times during my pregnancies. I'm sure if you're a mother you can relate. In Deuteronomy there is a verse that says, *"Blessed shall be the fruit of your womb and the fruit of your ground and the fruit of your cattle, the increase of your herds and the young of your flock."* (Deuteronomy 24:4). This is why it's so devastating when something happens to our children. It doesn't matter the level of the tragedy. The fear I believe stirs up in all of us is the same when we receive any type of news that has to do with our kids. Why is that? It's because as mothers we all share a special bond with our children that develops during pregnancy. A mother's love for her child has no ceiling to it. So, what do you do when you know a child is a gift from God and you have a child born with a birth defect, or who develops a terminal sickness or disease later in life? How does one prepare herself for the type of impact that is associated with each scenario?

As a mother I've been faced with the same questions that I just presented to you. I have three beautiful boys and with all three I've had to deal with some type of challenging situation at one time or another - whether it was inside the womb or a health issue that developed later in their lives. But God reassures us through his word that children are a gift. We must make one thing clear before we go any further, and that is with every good thing there's usually a hater somewhere lurking. Yes, I said, hater. God has a hater that entered this earth from the beginning of time. And since babies are from God, that means they too have an adversary, an enemy, and his name is Satan. He has one mission here on earth and that is to steal, kill, and destroy. He doesn't care if it's you, me, or even our kids. You might be thinking to yourself, I hear you Andrea, but where are you going with this? I have a child who was born with a birth defect or I have a child with a disease, and right now I'm afraid. Right now I'm feeling discouraged. I feel hopeless, I'm upset, and I'm angry. Why my child? Why my family? If this is you, know that all of your feelings and emotions are real and valid emotions and questions. It's the reason why I choose to talk about the enemy. Adversity is the host of spiritual warfare. Which is why I wanted to share this chapter from my book.

This prayer is for mothers who are all too familiar with, and can clearly relate to, what this chapter is about. My prayer is that this chapter breathes life, fight, hope, and encouragement into the mother who's carried and brought a child into this world that has a birth defect, sickness or disease, or the mother who is pregnant with a child, and has been told devastating news by the doctor. This prayer is to stand in the gap for mothers. I boldly speak to the birth defect and to that sickness or disease, and decree and declare Satan, NO MORE! You cannot, and you will not, disrupt the plans that God has for that baby boy's, or that baby girl's, life. God, you say in Your word, "For I know the plans I have for you," declares the LORD, "plans to prosper you and not to harm you, plans to give you hope and a future." (Jeremiah 29:11). In faith, and with courage rising up right now, I confidently stand on Your word with these women. Our Father in Heaven, wrap Your arms around this mother, breath into her comfort, peace and a renewed mind, a renewed way of thinking. Let her know You, and feel Your presence right there with her. Let her know that Your word is a lamp to guide her feet and a light for her path. (Psalm 119:105). Father, if she can no longer stand or walk, carry her, whisper in her heart with Your still soft voice, this too shall pass. What was meant for evil You'll make it good. Now with faith and boldness, women of strength scream, God will get the glory in Jesus name, amen!

Moms, I would like you to understand the word of God is very clear when it talks about how we "wrestle, not against flesh and blood, but against principalities, against powers, against the rulers of darkness of this world, against spiritual wickedness in high places." (Ephesians 6:12). This is Spiritual Warfare. I would like to encourage you to get a journal, put your child's name in it, and list the sickness, disease, or birth defect. Get intentional about this spiritual fight! Take back what belongs to you (Health). Spiritual War is the Christian concept of taking a stand against preternatural evil forces. It is based on the belief in evil spirits, which are able to disrupt human affairs. Many people believe that if they believe in God and have faith, they're exempt from trials and tribulations, or have a minimum of diabolic attacks. But this is untrue. The word of God is clear that we are not exempt from trials and tribulations when we give our lives to God. The Bible teaches us that it's the opposite. The good news is that when we are able to stand and endure our test, we learn how to persevere.

Allow me to take you into the most cherished, intimate parts of my life that have to do with me being a mother, and that is, my three sons. These boys are a huge reason why I fight to live each and every day. My sons, Tyrone Jr., Khai, and Kayden, have all experienced diabolical attacks from either the womb or later in their lives due to health issues. Through their spiritual warfare, faith and courage had to rise up in me. I had to learn how to fight spiritual battles, starting with my first-born son. My first pregnancy was one of the scariest times in my life, because it was not planned. On September 29th, on my husband's and father-in-law's birthday, I found out I was pregnant. I was instantly gripped with fear. I remember this news like it was yesterday. I thought it was the end of the world for me because I knew my life would change forever. My path as I understood it, was being altered. I was 20 years old with a list of goals that I had all written out. In this area of my life, I was goal driven. I also knew real quick that this child would trump them all for a time and that was disappointing to me. My ambition, determination and focus to finish school had to be put on hold. My husband, who was my boyfriend at the time, knew how focused I was with setting goals and keeping them a priority. Out of my fear and uncertainty and what I thought others would say, one of the first words out of my mouth was *abortion*! All my emotions were in disarray. I began to cry because although abortion screamed out from the inside of me, I knew deep down that answer was no. My high school sweetheart and I knew abortion wasn't the answer. Those words were being driven by fear. I thank God for Tyrone's courage to stand up for his child. He looked at me as he put his arms around me and he said, "I know you're afraid, but please don't abort my baby. I will do whatever it takes to provide for this baby and you." I could not ignore the sincerity and his opinion; after all, this was his baby, too. The conflict that weighed deep within my soul, my morals, and right from wrong, outweighed my fear. The decision was easy to make with his support. That night we were in agreement that I would have our baby. I remember the excitement and the joy that I felt. During my first prenatal appointment, you know the one where they do the ultrasound vaginally and you get to see the fetus for the first time on the monitor. I remember this day like it was yesterday. It was priceless! My baby was so active at seven weeks; this kid was doing somersaults. He was twirling around and jumping up and down. He looked like a stick figure cartoon character; I wish we had cell phones with video cameras because explaining it to you does it no justice. My heart filled with joy; I could not wait to meet this kid.

I would soon find out that to see him active like that would be significant for a huge decision later. After the nurse practitioner was done with the prenatal appointment, she had me go in a wheelchair from the clinic side to the hospital. The runner took me to a hospital room where I met a doctor who redid the ultrasound. This man's warm, welcoming spirit quickly turned into frustration and confusion, which led to him pouting and cussing. If you can imagine my joy turned into my heart beating fast with fear and confusion. When I asked him if everything was okay, he yelled out with many cuss words, "I'M NOT SURE." What he saw was bleeding outside the womb where the placenta had attached itself. His frustration and confusion was derived from his concern. He didn't know if this bleeding was from a blood clot or if I was hemorrhaging.

He didn't know if it would affect the supply or nourishment to the fetus or if the both of us were in danger. His response didn't make me feel good at all, so I asked him, "Does this mean that I would have to abort my baby?" He then used a few more choice words without giving me a clear answer and left out of the room. By this time my anxiety was through the roof. My eyes filled up with water and tears began to flow. That's when I heard this soft voice come from across the room. It was a lady who was my roommate who I had not seen in the hospital bed when I was wheeled into the room. I refer to her as my son's guardian angel! She said, "Excuse me, I don't mean to get in your business, but I overheard the doctor." She went on to ask me, "Do you want your child?" My response came with a little reluctance as the tears ran down my face, but my answer was yes, because what I had experienced prior to meeting this doctor was a happy, active baby that I could not wait to meet! This soft-spoken woman took an aggressive, but stern tone with me, and said, "Then you keep your baby, pray and trust God, everything is going to be fine." She went on to say, "Doctors don't always know everything." That was the game changer for me. Those words she uttered gave me the strength and encouragement to fight. If it wasn't for that lady, who knows what fear would have had me to do. I remember going home and talking to Tyrone about this upsetting day! He obviously could feel the fear and frustration through my voice. He knew in that moment I was afraid, but after I told him about the patient in my hospital room and what she said to me, he could also feel that I was hopeful. We were very much aware of the bleeding and unsure of the outcome and although this was an unsettling feeling, we adopted that childlike faith and together we got into agreement in prayer, and believed. We trusted God that our baby was safe and my body would be healed of the bleeding. When we prayed on our knees and believed in our hearts that we were fine, peace rested on us both.

I decided that I wanted a different doctor. So I reported that doctor to Kaiser and ended up with a new doctor. By my next prenatal and ultrasound appointment, the bleeding was completely gone. If fear would have had its way I might have gotten rid of my son, based on that doctor's response and fear of the unknown. But I said no, with a little intervention from that sweet lady. My new doctor, whom I loved, took over for the rest of my pregnancy. Even though they never could tell me where the bleeding was coming from, the rest of my pregnancy ended up being successful. I believed through prayer that God heard us. I carried him full term and gave birth to a healthy baby boy, Tyrone Jr.

Six years later I gave birth to another boy, named Khai. My whole pregnancy was a fight with Khai. If I had to put my experience to get Khai here into words, I would say the spiritual warfare was extremely intense. For the first time, I looked darkness and rulers of evil principalities in the whites of their eyes; everything that could come against me to bring him into this world came against me. It was a battle from the start. In my book, I go into greater detail, but to give you a glimpse, the start of this warfare started with my doctor. In this season of my life, my husband and I lived in Canada. My husband played professional football in this country for three and a half years. A few months before I became pregnant, after leading a very private life, it became public that my husband was released from the football team he was playing for. Dealing with the embarrassment, our family felt exposed, which brought on a severe case of depression. I worked part-time, but because of the stress of it all I had taken time off work because it was on the news almost every night for a week and I didn't want to answer any questions. My doctor knew how difficult this was for me, so she suggested that I take antidepressants. That didn't fly with my husband at all. He said, "NO!" He said, "You need to pray and go back to work and take walks." I thanked God that I listened because he was right. Returning back to work was the best decision for me. Now fast forward back to my doctor's appointment, my doctor said to me, as if my husband was not there in the room, "Are you sure you're ready for a baby? You guys just went through something very public." She then says, "Would you like to get an abortion?" The enemy would use that seed planted by my doctor later against me.

After that appointment my husband was so livid that she dismissed him as if he wasn't in the room. It was right around my seventh week when I developed hyper emesis, an extreme case of morning sickness where you are unable to keep anything down, which if not controlled can lead to severe dehydration. I passed out and ended up in the hospital. I was given nausea pills, but that didn't help. I was so sick that I ended back up in the hospital for a month before they decided to put a pic lined in my arm that's used for cancer patients. My doctor opted to give me a pic line so that my veins would stop collapsing from the IV bags. It also would allow for me to go home and have a nurse come daily to give me IV bags so that I could remained hydrated and hopefully keep food down. They set up a nurse to come in. My doctor reassured me that this would be great for me. That next day I was released from the hospital. It was a happy day for the Taylor family, until I received a phone call with some bad news. I was informed that day that I had fallen between the cracks. The ball had been dropped on me. I was told that I was out of the hospital's jurisdiction and that no nurse could come to our home. So what appeared at the time to be a disaster was enough to send me into a complete rage. Tears overtook me. I was frustrated. I felt miserable. I was so tired of being sick that I became resentful towards this baby. That day, I gave up. I told my husband to call my primary care doctor. I wanted an abortion. I was at my wit's end. I remember saying to myself,

"If this is how cancer patients feel every day then I see why they give up and die." I couldn't hold anything down; I mean absolutely nothing. When I was admitted for the second time into the hospital a GP doctor took me on as his patient and I knew he wasn't going to give me an abortion, but I knew who would. That's right, my primary care doctor. And that day she was who I called and left a message for.

Although this type of warfare was intense, many miracles happened throughout this whole pregnancy. On this day in particular God did some amazing things behind the scenes. That day my good friend from church heard of the news. She was a nurse at the hospital and asked if she could come to my house as a family member and teach my husband how to give me the IV bags daily. They said, "yes." Which was huge because the only other option was to go back into the hospital. She was able to do that and it was a blessing to us. Ty learn quickly how to give me my daily treatments to keep me hydrated.

I wish I could tell you that the warfare stopped there, but it only got worse. The warfare was so intense that I, as a mother, once I turned the corner and started feeling better I was able to see clearly. I prayed to God to forgive me for being resentful towards my child. I told God to get my baby here safely so I can hold him in my arms and protect him from the enemy.

About a week after Khai was born, my husband finished feeding him my breast milk through a bottle and he handed Khai back to me. Khai seem relaxed and content so I put him over my shoulder to burp him and something told me to look at him. I notice he looked like he wasn't getting much air; his eyes were out of focus and he began to choke. He could not get air. I stood up with him; I called his name, asking him if he was okay. I panicked, screaming what is wrong with him. I was so afraid because bubbles were coming out of his mouth while he was gasping for air. That's when I opened the front door completely panicked. I was ready to run down the street with him until Ty grabbed him out of my arms. Don't ask me where I was going. My thought process was, it's been hell this whole pregnancy and now that I have him in my arms feeling like I can finally protect him, I realize that the attacks are still present. I felt like, in that moment, I couldn't control what was going on. I questioned in my mind what was going on with my son.

My husband and I rushed him to Children's Hospital in Burnaby, Canada. This nurse called us in. She wanted to put an IV in his arm. I went around and around with her about putting an IV in his little arm at one week old. I didn't want to see him hurt. Finally, with tears in my eyes I said, "Go ahead." They admitted Khai into the hospital in the early hours of that Friday morning. This was the longest weekend. They did every test you could think of on him. I prayed like never before. When all the tests came back normal, I thought, *that's great, we'll be out of here Saturday morning*. The nurse informed me that the doctor wasn't releasing us until Monday! My heart sank because this was the same weekend Khai was going to be dedicated back to God. I could not understand if everything was normal why they wanted to keep him until Monday! The only answer that the nurse could tell me was that they wanted to monitor him for a few more days.

In my heart I took it very personally. Spiritually, I knew it was an attack from Satan. The Pastor that was supposed to dedicate Khai was moving to Africa and he was a mighty man of God. He could not wait to dedicate Khai and neither could I, but due to this attack we had to reschedule and the senior pastor ended up dedicating him at a later time. I wish I could tell you that the attacks stopped there but it was the beginning of an ongoing battle with spiritual warfare. In my book *The Cry Within: When prayer, the word of God and faith becomes the mandate*, I will revealed more of Khai's life in detail. It's been a journey. I would like to encourage you through my own personal spiritual warfare and experiences. If you have a child that's been afflicted in some way through a birth defect, sickness or disease, I would like you to know our kids were not born to be submitted to any illness, sickness or birth defect. You can choose to believe a different report, but know you will have to speak to it. What I've learned through my children's encounters with sickness, and diseases is spiritual warfare is real. Through my experiences I found out that every battle is different. Some demonic forces may leave with a simple prayer; where as other battles may require more. You may find you will have to dig your heels in deep, by fasting, praying, and speaking nothing but the word, like I've come to find out with my other two sons. These demonic forces, which are often referred to as a strong man or strongholds, usually come through the bloodline or can be associated with generational curses. That's exactly what happens later with my other two sons, Khai and Kayden. I go more in depth with in my book set to release in the spring of 2017. "The thief comes only to steal and kill and destroy; I have come that they may have life, and have it abundantly". (John 10:10).

Andrea Taylor-McCoy Bio:

Andrea Taylor is a Certified Christian Life Coach, a Career Coach, Author, Event Speaker, and CEO. Andrea is the founder of Present Yourself Proper, an organization for both teen girls and women. Andrea and her high school sweetheart, Tyrone Taylor, have been married since 2001 and are the parents of three handsome boys. She currently resides in the Bay Area.

Andrea enjoys coaching and teaching women weekly at Shepherd's Gate Women's Shelter. She hosts annual Girl Talk events, retreats, and workshops for teen girls and women.

Andrea's passion is to use her leadership skills and her life coach training to foster a safe place for teens and women to be transparent, vulnerable, and empowered so that they are free to grow personally, spiritually, and professionally into all they desire to be. Through her events, life coaching, teaching, and books Andrea's focus is to inspire teens and women to bring order back into their lives. Her mission is to "Bridge the Gap between young girls and women". Andrea understands "Empowered Girls, Empowers Lives."

Present Yourself Proper

Breaking Through
The Hurt!

I am not my Circumstances.
It was necessary!

By

Jamelia Jordan

Visionary ~ Entrepreneur ~ Event Manager & Designer ~

Travel Specialist ~ Heart for the people

jameliajordan@gmail.com

925-232-1206

Bay Point, CA

"Create the life you want and live the life you Love"

I thought that I was under a personal attack until I realized I was just under construction. I was given the challenge to learn how to love myself and love who GOD called me to be. How we love ourselves sets the stage for how we love and how we receive love from others. It is hard to both give and receive love when we don't actually know what it looks like.

<u>Discovering the Hurt</u>

It was my 35th birthday that I was preparing for. Determined to celebrate life and look as though I was the happiest person; however on the inside I didn't actually feel that way. I was in the mall a few days before my celebration of life "Little Black Dress Party" searching for something HOT to wear, something that will fit my personality and make me stand out. Everyone knows I love to dress and have a good time. As I am browsing inside of BEBE, this lady walked passed me and her reaction to me wasn't really pleasant. I was thrown off by her reaction. Her gesture and body language to me felt rather rude. I didn't know her so I immediately got offended by her presence.

Continuing to shop and trying not to pay her any attention, I noticed she kept walking past me, going back and forth until I finally asked if there was a problem. She replied, "No. I just got this strong vibe, your energy I felt something as I walked passed you." With a confused look on my face, I'm thinking,

"This woman is crazy and in about five seconds it's going to get real up in this store." She finally says, "Can I share something with you? I can only share if you agree to receive the information that I have to give you." Now I'm thinking this girl must want some money. I didn't have any money to give and if she is about to tell me I only have six months to live I did not want to know. Let me live my last six months the way I would without any expectations. She smiled and expressed that she didn't want any money and she wasn't going to tell me I was about to die; that is not how it works. Now I was only in the store to find me a dress, but I am so nosey that I became interested in what "Madame" had to say. I wanted to know if people really had the ability to read you and not know you from a can of paint. She goes right in and immediately says, "Honey you are a broken woman and you have been hurt really bad. You've been in this dark place for a very long time. You smile but it is just a cover up so people won't know the truth. You have people in your circle, family and friend that envy you. They are jealous and don't want to see no good come your way. You lack confidence in yourself; you don't believe in you. You have the heart of gold and the mindset of a wealthy person, but you continue to stand in your own way. Your pain is clouding your judgment."

This was more than enough information for me and I really wasn't convinced because it was very basic stuff. None of it was direct information; it could have been meant for anyone. I wear my emotions on my shoulders. So I am assuming the look on my face showed signs of uncertainty. We're standing in the middle of a clothing store and I just wanted to get my dress.

"Madame" suggested that we go to the coffee shop and have a seat because there was more. There's more if it wasn't personal to me; I wasn't sure I was interested. She says, "You've been worrying for a long time. Worry no more it's going to get better." She asked me, "Have you lost a lot of people who were close and dear to you within these last few years?" I replied, "Yes." She said, "You have a dark cloud over you and a shield covering you for protection." She then said, "You lost someone really close to you to violence about five years ago." At that moment I broke down into tears replying, "Yes, I lost my oldest brother on my mother's side when I was six months pregnant with my twins and it was devastating because eight years prior to that I had lost my father when I was six months pregnant with my son." "Madame" says, "Don't worry, your brother has you covered. The more you cry, the more you hurt, the more covering he provides. You have a dark cloud covering you and it represents a generational curse. I don't believe it was for you, however it's been following you prior to you being born. You were born broken."

After everything she had told me, I don't think I was fully convinced. I assumed she could feel that based off of my energy. So to add the icing on the cake, if I didn't fully believe, once she hit me with the most recent whammy I did. She says, "I am going to end with this. You had your heart broken recently. It was an indescribable pain by the very person you thought you would spend the rest of your life with. You trusted him with your entire being, but you came with a lot of baggage and so did he. Two broken people are a disaster waiting to happen. It would have never worked. Forgive, accept and move on. None of what you went through, or are going through, defines who you really are. You're destined for greatness and you're going to be ok emotionally, spiritually, physically, and financially. You will live the life you want, but in due time." That was nothing but God. He will use whatever resource He needs to use to open up your eyes when He wants your attention. From that point, I began to look at my life, where I came from and why things were the way that they were. I had been struck with the generational curse; I am BROKEN, I have ABANDONMENT issues, I have lost CONFIDENCE and I am faced with many INSECURITY issues.

Looking into my Past

I grew up in the house up until I was about ten years old, with just my mom and my two brothers and one sister. My mom and my dad were on and off, and most of the time she was more off and done with him, which was probably a good thing. They lived two very different lifestyles. My mom worked and was about taking care of her family, and my dad, well "Papa was a rolling stone" if you know what I mean. My dad had nine kids. Well I only hear and know of eight kids by four different women. So I didn't get to see that Mickey and Minnie kind of love within my own household. I grew up seeing what seemed to be a repeated cycle of back and forth relationships. No real monogamy; it was all about having your cake and eating it, too. As bad as I wanted for my mom and dad to become one, I always knew that the two were very different in the way that they lived their lives and it would never work. My mom was way too outspoken. No man or woman would ever be able to use her like a doormat and walk all over her. And if you got out of line, you might have caught one over the head. My dad was the ladies' man. In his mind, I'm guessing he was a player. He was always the life of the party and when I say life of the party, anything goes. Both my mom and dad had their differences and I can't speak for my other siblings, however, I can only speak for me. I was looking for that unconditional love a daughter receives from her dad; the kind of love where you are told on a daily how beautiful you are. I was looking for everything that I began looking for in relationships as I got older, realizing it should have been given to me as a child. My dad wasn't really in my life as he should have been. Mom had two girls with my dad. My sister and I always felt like we were the outsiders. It wasn't too often that we spent the time we should have with my father's side of the family because my mom wasn't taking us and if they wanted a relationship with us then my dad would be the one to make it happen. Someone from his side would have had to take the initiative to develop a relationship and bond with us. From time to time, there were certain uncles or cousins that would visit and come get us but that was only when the moon was blue. The relationship with my father's side didn't grow until I got older, from what I can remember. Can you say "BROKEN and ABANDONMENT ISSUES?" My older brother, whom I lived in the home with, was a significant person in my life; the only consistent male at that time that didn't not leave.

Later in my childhood, a new sheriff came into town and I thought I would finally get to see my mom get that MICKEY and MINNIE love. They dated, and dated, had a child, and dated some more for years. At that time he became the only male role model that we knew. Although I was hoping for marriage, which never happened, he played a significant role in our lives. I look back now; that was not enough. I see so much greatness in my mom. That same greatness I see in her was instilled in me. We go day to day without recognizing it ourselves.

My mom is the protector and the provider. She's the head of the house and sometimes living in the house with her I felt like I was in the MILITARY. She kept us in church and for years I was in church, but church wasn't in me. I felt like my mom was so hard on me, as if I could never get anything right. A lot of the times I felt like the black sheep of the family. So I grew up feeling like I had to prove to myself that I am GREAT. Don't get me wrong; my mom is a hard working woman. She took care of five kids with little to no support, by herself. She raised not only her kids, but she opened her doors to her siblings' children, friends' children, and foster care. She poured so much into others I think she forgot to pour into herself. Guess WHAT? That is the woman I am today. If I could turn back the hands of time, I would have had a more personal, intimate relationship with my mom. A relationship where I wasn't afraid to share my deepest, darkest secrets without wondering what she would think of me. I know she was then, and is now, proud of all my accomplishments. But hearing "JOB WELL DONE" every now and then would have made a world of a difference. I struggle when it comes to relationships, friends, family, and dating. I realize that if I knew then what I know now, I could have saved myself a lot of heartaches and pain. I would be able to weather the storm a lot easier than I have, at least that's what I'm thinking.

Recognizing The Hurt

Here I am, in my mid 30's, three kids and three failed relationships, where I thought each one was *the one*. I could not wait to be acknowledged as an adult and make decisions for myself. After graduating from high school, I became a party girl. I stayed running the streets. Oh, and yes, just like my daddy, I was the life of the PARTY! At a college party in my 20's I met a guy, Chocolate Drop is what my auntie called him. We talked, we hung out, we FELLOWSHIPPED. In my head, he was my boyfriend because I had given him all of me. No, No, it doesn't work like that. You're really just another notch on that man's belt. After hanging for some time, we came up with this bright idea to have a baby. He gave me this spiel about how I would make a great mom. He could see us developing a future together, blah, blah, blah. Now I never wanted any kids, but it was something about Chocolate Drop; I was all in. Did we have a relationship? I can't say yes for sure, but I can say out of the five years I dealt with him the best thing that came from it was my son. My first LOVE! There was a lot of back and forth with this situation-ship. The lying, cheating, and deceiving. This went on for years and him having another baby didn't stop me from chasing behind him.

It wasn't until we got into a physical altercation, I DON'T DO DOMESTIC, that it was time to go. That relationship was dead. I thought I knew what heartbreak felt like and that I learned my lesson, but I didn't.

In a matter of months, I went from one relationship to another. I wasn't really in church, so I did not have the covering I needed. I was in and out, straddling the fence because I was learning that church folks were some of the biggest hypocrites. When I found out I was pregnant with my son, the mothers in the church sat me down because I wasn't married. I didn't understand, so I figured I didn't need to go to church if I had a relationship with God. Five months after my situation-ship, I was single and ready to mingle. And because my flesh was weak, I went looking for Mr. Right. That's when I met my Teddy Bear. Over time he, too, became the love of my life. Once again, giving another man the same benefits you would give your husband. I had given him all of me and I was just his girlfriend! I was trying to make something of this relationship because I didn't want to start over, and although the RED FLAGS were there, I ignored them. This went on for a few years and OOPS what do we have now? We have the twin girls and a man who walked away because he wasn't ready and needed to get his life together. REALLY!

At this point, I am done. I am not dating. I am focusing on my kids and me. I'm going to start working on my relationship with

God, blah, blah, blah. It had been a year since the twins' arrival. I was chilling, not looking for anything, just getting me together. I was minding my own business, went hanging out with my friend to have a little fun time and I met a guy. I wasn't really interested but he was cool. We talked, we hung out, and over time, the love bug hit me. Once again history was about to repeat itself. Eventually, we cohabitated and here I am living like a family, playing the role of a wife without the title. A title I thought I wanted so badly. A few years later, the same person I loved the most was the very person to break my heart and suck the life out of me. It was as if I was living in this alternate universe when it all transpired. I'm thinking, how in the HELL can someone profess they love me, be a father to my daughters, friend and role model to my son and after spending a few years together, suddenly he walk away? There were some issues, but I guess love had me blind. He had come on so strong and determined to acquire my love. Was I perfect? No, but neither was he. I thought I had found my BOAZ, my life partner, and sadly in the early hours of September 2014, it was all over. It didn't make sense to me; nothing to me added up. I constantly asked myself what was going on. Didn't I finally do it right? What about my kids? No, he wasn't the father but he played a significant role. We had our differences, yes, but I thought the love was strong enough to fight through and grow through. For a long time I was angry, hurt, and confused. My kids were torn because I was torn. I was so focused on everything but the right things, which was getting me together so that I could be the MOM my kids needed. Trying to manage the hurt, I realized that I was grieving a loss. This was an indescribable pain that I had never felt. But, if I was aware of who I was and Whose I was, my suffering would not have lasted as long as it did.

Many weeks, days, long nights of crying and praying, and thanking God for a circle of friends, family and my spiritual sister's support. Without them, I don't know where I'd be. I'm thankful for the tough love, encouraging words, and truthful moments we had. I needed it all. I realized I depended so much on him being there that I had forgotten how to live without man and trust God. I was dying in the meantime. My life was falling apart physically, emotionally, financially, and I was spiritually disconnected. What was I teaching my kids? I didn't think I could live without him, but look at God! It was time to put my big girl pants on and work on self. I began to love me.

When I accepted what was, the Holy Spirit spoke to me. I heard Him tell me the reasons why He allowed the breaking of my relationship. While the words were shocking, I accepted them and meditated on them for a long time afterwards. This is when I realized I was being selfish in my spirit and the Lord had revealed to me that I had once again placed a man of mine so high in my heart that I'd begun to idolize him. Without even realizing it, I had given him the throne of my heart. He lived there in my thoughts, emotions, and actions. That man was reigning over me and all along I didn't have a clue. Yes, we had our differences, No, I didn't always show my love, but I didn't really know what love looked like. What I did know was that he was my everything, so I thought. News Flash! I had to learn the hard way. We all know that if we put anything before God, we will lose it. So, I lost the love of my life (or at the time whom I'd foolishly given the title to). Yet, in the middle of it all, I gained a brand new perspective and uncovered my purpose in Christ. Growing through that life-changing experience made me feel as if I were so far from the person that I'd known myself to be. Through the remnants of a broken heart I had started on a journey that would take me into another realm of life.

I can't stress how important it is for you to HEAL before you DEAL. You don't want to become the bag lady. If I was in a better place in my life and if my relationship with God was solid before that painful experience, who knows what the results would have been. Even in my pain I was being blessed and didn't know it. I learned that the breakup isn't always a bad thing. I grew to know that there is a blessing in every lesson, as the songwriter Eryka Badu would say. I realized I had become so complacent that I didn't value my self-worth. It took God to remove some things and people out of my life. It wasn't to take away my happiness, but to show me it was never supposed to be. I was ignoring all the signs so He let me entertain it for a while, but in order for my permanent to arrive, He had to remove it. Yes it hurt, stung and to me it was unfair, but IT HAD TO HAPPEN. IT WAS NECESSARY.

Just like Abraham and Lot, some people and things are not designed to continue with you on your journey. I had to learn to let go and walk away from those doors that God had closed. That job. That person. That Material. That Habit. That Money. Bad Memories. The Past. Insecurities and Fear. It all had to go because, while I was making my mistakes, I was breaking God's Heart. The most tragic thing in the world is not death, but life without reason. It is dangerous to be alive and not know why you are given life. The enemy almost had me. He definitely played on my weakness, but my God was bigger than my struggle. I've learned to forgive myself and be happy for others.

I am at the point in my life where it's time to stop prostituting my emotions and the decisions I make in my life to please anyone other than GOD! I am the definition of Love, Hope, and AMBITION. I am Every Woman!

I am focusing on me learning how to let go of the past. Releasing all of the baggage I've carried along the way. The hurt, not just from relationships, but the hurt I've received from family, friends, and businesses. It is time to just LET IT GO! I've asked God in His time when He is ready to send me a strong man, a praying man to help build me up because I am a broken women going through the process of healing. I am in labor with my purpose. The pains that I have endured hurt so much that it is all uncomfortable for me, but in the end I know it will all be worth it. I am entering into a new season in my life and my labor won't be easy. The doctor said he can see the head but the pressure is so painful at times, I don't think I can handle it. I heard him say, "Just one more Big Push and you will be able to see the fruit of your labor." So pray for me as I breathe in and do this last PUSH! Knowing that my circumstances don't determine my future. Loving that I had to go through to grow through. And I am growing into a new being and I know that everything of values takes time. God is showing me daily what LOVE, and I mean unconditional LOVE, really looks like. So everything I thought was great. I know God has something greater.

Jamelia Jordan Bio:

Born in San Pablo, California, November 1980, into a big family of six sisters and four brothers. She is a proud mother of six-year-old twin girls and a fourteen-year-old young man whom are the joy of her life. She graduated from the University of Phoenix with a Bachelor of Science in Business Management/Marketing. Later she attended Full Sail University achieving a Masters of Arts Degree in Entertainment Business with a focus on Advance Business Law.

In 2013, God gave her the vision to become her own BOSS by birthing the idea to start up her own full service Event Management Company, "Decadence Defined." Jamelia Jordan is the CEO of Decadence Defined, a full service event planning/design and travel management lifestyle company; a positioning and branding company that gives exceptional planning and designs to events. Later in 2014, she decided to expand her event planning company and add travel management which birthed "Decadence Destinations" the sister company to Decadence Defined.

Jamelia feels she was born a visionary and entrepreneur, with a millionaire mindset. She has a heart to inspire others to get what they need out of life. Her mission in life is to dream, achieve and be a GOAL DIGGER not a GOLD DIGGER. She wants to live life in abundance and never in lack. She strives to create the life she wants so that she can leave a legacy for generations to come. Her motivation is her children. Jamelia is dedicated to making them proud to call her "MOM". She is a lover of God and strives to walk in the life of a Proverbs 31 woman. There are many times she wanted to give up, however, the heart and fight in her would not allow her to do so. Her favorite saying is "I may have lost the battle, but I will WIN the WAR!"

My Mess Turned
Into My MESSage!

A Banana and a Prayer

By

Taliah Jonee' Johnson

Training Specialist ~ Singer ~ Songwriter ~ Speaker

Email: Info@TaliahJonee.com

www.TaliahJonee.com

Vallejo, CA

I entered August 2005 preparing for my senior year of college at *The* Dillard University (est. 1869) in New Orleans, LA. I was full of excitement and pride. How I loved my HBCU! I loved the gleaming white of the buildings, the green grass, and the humidity in the air. I loved the slowness of the city. Coming from the hustle and bustle of the Bay Area, I found comfort in slowing down. I loved the rod iron fence that seemed to encamp around us as we safely grew into change agents in the bosom of our beloved university. I loved my classmates. We were family. We were loved and protected as we learned life lessons, achieved goals and stepped out of our comfort zones, all as the breeze moved through the branches of our majestic oak trees persuading them to sway to and fro as if they were dancing to zydeco. My love for my school ran deep. I had begun to find myself, and see myself, as an adult after moving off campus into a little house with two good friends. Yes, this was me, and I was here for all of it. I was ready to walk down the famous Avenue of the Oaks come May 2006 and lay my eyes on the prize I diligently worked for. My degree. My sheepskin as my grandmother called it. My first taste of success.

Oh, New Orleans. The multicolored shotgun houses, the We Never Close po'boy shop, the Garden District, the street cars on St. Charles, chocolate children on the RTA (Or the 'Rita) city bus in their catholic school uniforms, the Wing Shack off

Claiborne, the Esplanade Mall, the Superdome, the West Bank, the bounce music, the uptown, the downtown, the second lines that would process outside campus and abruptly stop lecture as those of us from out of state would run to the windows to marvel at how they celebrated their loved ones on their way to their final resting place. The hospitality of the people, the accent, the love, the hue, the Quarter, the beignets, the riverboats, the 5-0-4.

My mother and I drove my car down to New Orleans from the Bay Area and it was quite an adventure. We'd high five and celebrate as we crossed each state line on the way there. We laughed, sung Anita Baker's greatest hits, and enjoyed one another's company as we drove cross country like Thelma and Louise. As we arrived in New Orleans, it felt like the beginning of a dream. I was so happy to share the beginning of this season with my mommy. The reunions with my roommates were as dramatic as the last scenes from The Color Purple! We laughed, cried, and expressed our excitement for the year that was to be our best yet. My mom filled our fridge, as moms tend to do, and we hugged and said our goodbyes as she boarded a plane to go back home and I started to mentally prepare to kill it in the classroom.

The first week was pretty easy. Some of my classes were cancelled and that allowed me more time to mix and mingle with my fellow classmates and Tasha, who was my right hand in leadership over our school's section of the National Council of Negro Women, as we planned out a year that was to be EPIC for us! Yes, I was opening up, spreading my wings, coming into my own and loving it. The weather was absolutely beautiful and we were excited to be reunited again. The excitement was tangible and contagious.

Saturday, August 27, 2005. I woke up to my phone ringing. It was my grandfather in Baton Rouge, about an hour north of New Orleans. He sounded concerned. *"Good morning, Papa,"* I said groggy and dazed. *"You need to get out of New Orleans and come to Baton Rouge. That hurricane is going to hit and I want you out of the city."* I looked outside. The sun was shining, the sky was a beautiful blue and there were no clouds in sight. I responded, *"Papa, remember last year when they said Hurricane Ivan was going to hit and devastate the city? Remember how nothing happened? This is the same thing! It's going to be fine, don't worry."* He hung up on me, but not before he told me that he was going to call my dad in an effort to convince me to pack a bag and leave the city until the storm blew over. My phone rang again, and sure enough, it was my dad. I'm still in the bed wishing they would stop worrying! My dad tried to convince me to leave as well, but I wasn't budging. We hung up and right after that a friend called from California telling me he thought I needed to leave as well. *"What is everyone so worried about?"* I thought to myself.

As I started moving through the house, I settled onto the couch and my phone rang again. This time it was a good friend from school. She was crying. Her family decided they weren't going to leave and she was terrified and she told me that she wanted to leave the city. I started to get concerned. *"Let me turn on the news"* I thought. I turned the channel to find mayors and city leaders pleading with the residents in their Parishes to leave. Local government officials were in tears reading instructions on how to contact emergency resources should the need arise. Giving routes and directions on where to seek shelter should leaving be impossible for some in the area. Still on the phone with her, I told her to pack a bag and I come with me to Baton Rouge since my grandfather was waiting on me anyway. She agreed and we hung up. I still believed that everyone was overreacting. *"Nothing is going to happen but I'll just pack a few things and go out there so she and grandpa can feel better,"* I thought.

I packed 2 outfits, flip flops, and 1 church outfit in a tote bag. Just enough for the weekend. I figured there was no need to bring more than that since we'd be right back on Sunday night. As I was leaving, I had my cell phone in one hand and a banana in my other hand. I walked through our living room to the front door and I prayed, *"Lord, even if there is a hurricane*

– which I don't believe there will be – but even if there is, I pray that you let this be the only house left standing on the block. In Jesus' name, Amen." I walked out the door, locked it and made my way to my friend's apartment. As I drove past a gas station on the way there, I saw a line of cars lined up and down the block waiting for gas. *"That's odd,"* I thought. It still hadn't sunk in. I picked up my friend and we made it to Baton Rouge in about an hour. Later, I found out that had we left just an hour later, it would have taken us anywhere from six to eight hours to get there. People were running out of gas on the interstate, stuck in the heat and humidity with no water, no restroom, etc. Having just missed the chaos and totally oblivious to what was happening around us, we went shopping. Buying clothes and talking about the upcoming school year. We finally made it to my grandfather's house and though he was irritated that we went to the mall, he was relieved that we'd made it safely.

Sunday, August 28th was very quiet. We spent the day talking about our goals for the school year and checking in with friends and family letting them know where we were and that we were safe and sound. We were ready to return back to school but we agreed to stay as the news coverage advised all residents to remain where they were as a precaution. By this time, I thought that it would be a bad storm, but nothing more. I don't think anything could have prepared me for what was to happen the next day.

On Monday, August 29th I was awakened by my cell phone ringing. It was a friend from home. "Are you ok?" he asks. "Yes, I'm fine," I say as I wake up and hear the wind and rain bashing against my grandfather's house. I sit up in the bed, "Why?" I ask. "Because the hurricane is over New Orleans right now." I freeze. I stopped breathing. "What do you mean??" I hung up the phone and ran into the living room. My friend was already in the living room watching. Crying. Totally confused as I realized that a real live hurricane had touched down over New Orleans. This is happening. Hurricane Katrina was in full effect. Right now. We sat in silence for a long time as the storm ravaged Baton Rouge and Katrina laid waste to our beloved 5-0-4.

We couldn't get in contact with anyone with a 5-0-4 area code. We had no idea where people were, if they got out, etc. I had no idea where my roommates were, she couldn't get in contact with her family in the city, and we were terrified. There was no coverage in the city initially so we didn't know what was left of our beloved school or our neighborhoods. What is happening? Why is this happening? Finally they began letting cameras into the city – aerial views initially. I was on the phone with my brother as we watched the coverage live. They panned over the Gentilly neighborhood, over the University of

New Orleans, and over Lake Pontchartrain, and the homes in between these landmarks looked as if they were simply roofs lying in a body of water. Our house was in this neighborhood. Roofs in water were what was left. I broke. I went hysterical. Gone. I'm seeing it right now, live on TV everything is gone. I had only packed 2 outfits. Everything else was in water. Everything changed.

What do we do now? We decide to drive to Houston to fly back home, her to Bay Saint Louis, MS, and me to Vallejo, CA. We can't find our friends. We don't know what's going on with our school. Our belongings have been destroyed. It's time to go home. I drove her to the airport and I stayed the night with a cousin, as my flight was leaving the next morning. I remember lying on a pallet in her floor in tears. Remembering the Avenue of the Oaks. The gleaming white buildings. Our little house. Our friends. Outside of us, what about our neighbors? Our beloved New Orleans community? *"Lord, what is happening?"* Seeing the coverage of people sitting outside of the convention center, looting, etc., made me sick. *"My people. Why isn't anyone helping?"* It was almost too much to handle. I can remember getting so worked up that I'd randomly burst into tears at the thought of all I had just experienced and worrying about those still struggling to survive after such devastation.

I was traumatized. Seeing those run down homes, images of the dead, and fear of what could have come of us haunted me as I slept every night. I was lost and unsure of my future. After some mental stillness, I agreed to return to the job I'd held during the summer months. I was still sorting through my thoughts and feelings about finishing school, and with my heart still with DU I didn't think I was ready to finish. I thought I needed a break. But one morning I was awakened with a jolt of motivation. *"Your Caucasian competition is waking up and getting it done. You need to get your behind in the classroom."* With that, I enrolled at Holy Names University in Oakland, CA, as they were taking in students displaced by the hurricane.

In January 2006, the beginning of my second semester, a good friend shared with me that her father was planning to visit New Orleans to check on his mother's home. She also lived in the Gentilly area and though I was convinced that all was lost I gave her father my house key and asked that he just go by to confirm what I had already known. He agreed and said he'd let me know if the damage was significant, or if it was worth my while to recover what was left. I thanked him for the effort, though I was sure he'd say that it wasn't worth my time to gather up what had been damaged or looted through. I wasn't holding my breath.

I was at work in mid-January when my cell phone rang. I answered, *"Hello?"* I said apprehensively. *"Hi, it's dad. I'm here at your house and you can come get all your things."* I stopped breathing. *"I'm sorry, what do you mean all my things?"* I was confused. I saw the roofs lying in the water in Gentilly. I saw the University of New Orleans and I saw the Lake on TV. We lived right in between the two. Surely our house was destroyed. He clarified, *"Yeah I see how the water rose onto the property, but it didn't get past the porch. If it had, with you having wood floors, the floors would've buckled and the house would've caved in. Everything seems to be working, the lights, the TV. The only problem is that the food in the fridge has rotted."* I was stunned. I thanked him and ran to the bathroom in the office and gave God all the glory in my bathroom stall. Tears streaming down my face, hands lifted and feet dancing because God had blown my mind. I couldn't understand why or how our house was spared. Then God took me back to that little crazy prayer I prayed with the cell phone in one hand and the banana in the other. He honored it. He left our house standing. The water hadn't even gotten past the porch. Beyond that, it hadn't been broken into. From August 2005 to January 2006 our house had been untouched. It was then that I realized that God's protection is real and is activated when we pray in faith. Even if our prayers are small and insignificant to us. A mustard seed is all we need. I remember through my tears asking Him, *"So all you wanted was for me to move home? You spared everything! So all this was for me was a change of scenery?!"*

125

I traveled down to New Orleans at the end of January. It was cold and a good part of the city was still without power so any recovering I did had to be done during the day because it was dangerous to be out at night. People were trying to survive and breaking into homes for food and other supplies. It was an emotional trip. Driving through the neighborhoods that I had become accustomed to and seeing the damage. Seeing the symbols spray-painted on the homes indicating bodies had been found. My Lord, please send your spirit. *"God, I'm grateful for this blessing you granted us, but I'm hurting for those who lost their lives and loved ones and all their possessions. There were houses on our block that were destroyed but you spared us. How? Why?"*

I sat in the car in the driveway totally blown away. Staring at the house that looked exactly how I remembered it. Not sure what to expect, I walked into our house and sure enough everything was as we left it. God is amazing. The license plate holder my mom bought me when things were simple and my senior year was still ahead of me was still sitting on my dresser in the same exact spot. Amazing. God literally kept me. Kept me all the way from New Orleans, to Baton Rouge, to Houston, to Vallejo, to this moment. His recovery game is on point. I cried in my bedroom. Fell down to my knees in disbelief. I just knew all was lost. I recalled getting off the plane with a tote bag of my things thinking that everything was gone, and all along He used that season to show me just how powerful He is.

I tell this story to encourage you. You may be thinking that what you're going through will destroy you, but God is just moving some things around! He's saying, *"Let me give you a change of scenery!"* If you are reading this and feel that all is lost, I want you to know that you are not forgotten! You will survive. God will send His angels to have charge over you, *'Lest you dash your foot against a stone' (Psalm 91:12).* Please trust His plan for your life. A mustard seed of faith is all you need. God's recovery game never disappoints. You will win. His Word says so. Be encouraged my sister and my brother. Victory shall be yours.

Holy Names University Graduate, Cum Laude, 2006. God did it.

Taliah Johnson Bio:

Taliah Johnson is a wife, a mother and an author living in the San Francisco Bay Area. With a successful blog (mommymusings03.wordpress.com), Taliah writes under the pen name Joneé Writes where she provides her perspective on motherhood, friendship, marriage, and being a woman of color using comedy, spirituality and personal anecdotes. Through her writing, she desires that the reader laugh with her, cry with her, and see themselves in her journey as she writes from her lens.

Having graduated from Holy Names University (Oakland, CA - Business Management) and the American Baptist Seminary of the West (Berkeley, CA -Masters of Divinity), Taliah worked in the corporate office of a financial institution for a number of years, and participated in leading children's, youth and young adult ministries for a number of years as well. She has a heart for people and thrives in the company of others who are also committed to living lives devoted to self-reflection, self-improvement, and self-forgiveness.

By sharing her triumphs and blunders as a Christian, a woman, a wife, and a mother, Taliah wants the reader to *"Be strong and find encouragement in the fact that you are not alone."* She uses her stories to illustrate that even with all you've gone through, you can still be used of God to be a blessing to others. Through her honesty, she emphasizes that we must be able to laugh at ourselves. Life is too short. You are not damaged goods. You can still make yourself proud even though you've encountered rough waters on your voyage to self-love and acceptance.

Taliah and her wonderful husband Kristofer are blessed to do life together with their beautifully gifted daughters, Ava and Zola.

I am not a Victim,
I am a Victor!

An Empty Void That Was Finally Filled

By

Deidra Jackson-Middleton

Age: 26

Author ~ Administrative Assistant II/ Lab Associate

Antioch, CA

Contact info: Deidracali@gmail.com / 510-395-6402

Having low self-esteem and not having a voice of my own, has put me in life compromising situations. Unselfishly, I focused more on pleasing others rather than acknowledging my own feelings; which produced self-inflicted wounds and sometimes jeopardized my safety. My mom did an amazing job with teaching me strong morals and the importance of inner beauty, but somewhere along the way I picked up insecurity. While staring in the mirror I often tore myself apart, embracing the strong void that became a piece of me as I carried on with not being sure of whom I was. All along I hadn't realized that I was suffering from emotional and physical neglect from my biological father disappearing to where the phone calls and visits became infrequent. My teenage mind couldn't fathom the seed that had been planted and its roots being the main cause of my fallible decisions or lack thereof. I thrived off the feeling of being wanted and became crazy about the idea of love, and the security it brings. I was pained by rejection. Looking back I noticed that my innocence vanished at the age of 14, while searching immensely for my love cup to be filled.

The desire to be esteemed and feel the affection and importance from a man only intensified as I realized it was attainable through dating. Having a childhood was extremely important to my mother who had a hard time overcoming her childhood being stolen at an early age. She was very overprotective and militant and dating was off-limits. She protected me from those that preyed on the young; although little did I know the error of my own ways would lead me right onto the course of wretchedness. And having to always need validation and lacking confidence led me in the arms of wolves dressed as sheep.

Essentially, I only became interested in the older guys, but wasn't fully aware of the can of worms I was opening. Often I felt indiscernible and I was tremendously shy and quiet in the presence of a guy because I didn't feel like I was ever enough. I always ended up dating someone who was never a person I'd chosen out of assurance; instead I'd date them by default; just because they liked me. It didn't even matter what their qualities were or if they weren't attractive. I needed to feel loved and have their undivided attention. My emotional hurt was deeply embedded and I couldn't find its source.

My older brother was an up and coming rap artist and he used to invite his friends over who were like-minded individuals. One day an acquaintance of his, Rell, had visited the house and they were making music in the garage. I had seen this guy before from around the way but I never met him. Little did he know I was secretly infatuated with him and intrigued by his demeanor. He wasn't as attractive in the face. The only discouraging factor was my age; so I thought. He was nineteen years old at the time and I was barely turning fourteen years old. Getting involved with an older guy wasn't on my agenda, but I did not oppose. I was extremely book smart and held a 4.0 grade point average, but when it came to boys I was passive and naive. Trying my hardest to disassociate my age from my appearance, I held a high standard of maturity, which couldn't compare to someone with experience. Though honoring what my mother said was in my nature, this desperation I felt was beyond my control. Even though I knew I wasn't ready for what came with dating an older guy, it wasn't enough to hold me back. Curiosity was seeping out of the bag.

The saying, "A hard head makes a soft behind", was very true in my case. Fat meat was undeniably greasy. One of my sister's friends named Morgan would stay overnight at the house all the time, and we became really close. She was four years older than me but you couldn't tell the age difference. Morgan happened to know Rell and reached out to a mutual friend. She called him up with the intentions of letting him know who I was and that I was interested in him and to see what he felt about it. He seemed a little apprehensive at first but then he said he wanted to set something up for us to meet.

When I met Rell he seemed very genuine and sweet, he hung around my sister's boyfriend so I had become familiar with their lifestyle. The dynamic of our conversation was captivating, but immediately when the conversation came up about sex I let him know that I was a virgin and was not interested in changing that anytime soon. His response was shocking when he said he would wait for as long as he needed to. Everyone around us felt as though the relationship was safe because of him expressing his patience and his willingness to wait for me. Our beginning was very slow, but I was comfortable with that pace.

A month or so after we begin to talk he asked me to be his girlfriend and professed that he was starting to fall in love with me. He then began bringing sex back into our conversations and saying if I loved him and planned on being with him, and only him, then it shouldn't be so hard to try it out. I felt backed into a corner. I knew I wasn't ready to allow him to have my virtue, but I entertained the conversation. I was extremely inexperienced and knew nothing about sex. But he kept pressing the issue and soon his behavior started to change. At times he made it seem as though he was mad at me and would hang the phone up in my face because I wouldn't sneak out or do the things he had asked me to do. He started showing very manipulative behavior and I often fell for it. I would ask for rides just to go meet him at his house and see him for a few minutes. People that knew about us became concerned, but I reassured them that I was fine.

The longer we were acquainted the more his true colors started to show. One night he had asked me to sneak out and I did. We had gone to one of his friend's house and he told me we were just going to talk. He ended up pursuing me and told me that if I loved him I would show him. Though I said no and hesitated, I gave him what he wanted because I didn't want to disappoint him and hear that he'd been with someone else. Things ended quickly that night due to me being uncomfortable and he took me back home. Rumors started surfacing of him seeing other girls and I was hearing gossip of me not being a virgin anymore, which made me really upset and distant. I ran into him one day and he told me that the rumors were false and that he was no longer talking to other girls. I believed him because I didn't want to risk losing the man that loved me.

During that summer my auntie went to Colorado for a vacation, and my sister and I asked our mom if we could stay the night with my cousin for the week, and my mom was ok with it. Rell and his friends came over and we all laughed and joked around. Later on that night, Rell and I were watching a movie and we conversed for hours about our goals and aspirations. He told me that he was going to take care of me and reassured me that his intentions weren't to hurt me and that he saw us having a future. I kept an open-mind about the dynamics of our relationship, but everybody could see I was extremely unreceptive of reality when it came to him. I did what he wanted and kept our relationship a secret from my mom; he was the first guy that I loved. All I wanted was to feel chosen and valued. My problem was that I was a typical young minded girl, and knew nothing about my own value or self-worth. It was hidden behind the shadow of this man. I knew I had no business being in this situation, but it was as though my inner voice spoke when my physical voice wouldn't and unfortunately I didn't listen nor use either one.

Warning Comes Before Destruction

The next night things were different. My mom had called to check in on my sister and I, but we asked her if we could stay for a few more days. Rell had come over again and our conversation had progressed into physical contact; he pressured me about trying things out again. After the night before, we felt closer, as if we connected intellectually. I couldn't believe that I had put myself in this situation once more; I didn't speak up for myself. My gut feeling was telling me to end things quickly and to tell him how uncomfortable sex made me feel, but instead I went along with it. After everyone had gone to sleep he made his move and this time he grabbed protection and proceeded; to him my "no" meant "yes". I was so apprehensive and my body tensed up, but I managed to compromise with his request. I started to come to my senses and realized this wasn't what I wanted to do. I began to tell him to stop but he was resistant and zoned out as if I hadn't said a word. And I noticed he became extremely rough and went full force. He didn't respond. I said it louder and more firmly, "Stop", and he ignored me. He became very aggressive and handled me as if I was experienced sexually just as much as he was. Then I noticed a puddle of wetness beneath me and it alarmed me. I told him to get off me once more and he must have heard the panic in my voice and got up. When he turned on the lights we saw that there was blood everywhere. I had already had my monthly cycle and my flow was never as heavy. I immediately went to the bathroom and a trail of blood followed. I put on a sanitary napkin and I felt pain all in my stomach area. He asked me if I was ok but I was so pissed off at him and upset with myself for getting into this predicament, I didn't answer. How could I have let this happen? I began to condemn myself. He apologized. Horrified with all the blood, I laid down and checked periodically hoping that the bleeding would stop. By the time morning came he was gone and off to work. I went to the bathroom and saw that the bleeding hadn't stopped; I bled through everything including the furniture. I got into the shower and the blood and clots ran down my legs nonstop, uncontrollably; I began to panic.

I told my older cousin, sister, and friend what had happened and they were afraid that we would all get in trouble. So I called the advice nurse and Planned Parenthood to ask them what to do. They all recommended that I go to the emergency room immediately. My sister and cousin were in disbelief; they became angry with him. By this time I had been bleeding for over eleven hours straight and I begin to feel dizzy and faint. I told my cousin and my sisters that I didn't care about facing the consequences from our parents; my life was now in danger. I needed medical attention right away. So we gathered our things and begin walking down the stairs. My eyesight faded and everything became black. I was in and out and losing my breath. We made it to the car and I begin to wheeze heavily and gasped for oxygen. I was so scared. I couldn't breathe and I saw black once more. I remember asking God silently, "Please do not let me die!" That was the first time I recalled God showing up right away. My cousin started driving faster, and instantaneously God breathed the breath of life back into my body and my vision was restored.

We arrived to the hospital and a trail of blood clots fell through my sweats, and without hesitation, I was taken into triage. A host of medical staff surrounded me and asked me tons of questions, such as was I raped and what had transpired. They couldn't stop the bleeding. I was lying there hemorrhaging as blood clots the size of golf balls came out. I prayed even harder. My cousin was in the room crying profusely; she couldn't take seeing me like that. I remember her being so regretful and apologetic that this had happened, but I didn't blame her. I was young and looking for love and acceptance in all the wrong places and walking in my disobedient ways, which left me fighting for my life. Since I was a minor, it was hospital protocol to call my guardian. Boy, was I extremely nervous, but at the moment I couldn't entertain the anxiety. My mom came in with tears filling her eyes asking me if was I ok. I didn't want to tell her truth, but she deserved to know.

By the time my mother came in I was so drained and weak from so much blood loss that I was getting IV fluids. The doctor said I would do fine without a blood transfusion but declared that I was now anemic and must be put on iron pills. They managed to stop the bleeding. She allowed me to sleep and rest, but when she came back into the room I began to explain the situation. I lied about who the person was, just so that he wouldn't go to jail. My mom was appalled by my actions and the fact that I nearly died and was covering up for this person who obviously didn't give two cares for me. The news that I was in the hospital spread like wildfire. Rell was informed while he was at work; everybody began to question him about what really happened. He lied and tried to cover his side of the story, and was telling my friend who was there, to tell me that I better not say anything.

My mom was sick to her stomach after it was confirmed through word of mouth that it was Rell. She knew his step dad and he begged my mom not to go to the authorities. She went to Rell's mother's house and told her everything. The streets were talking and making up more stories as they fabricated the truth and added on empty lies. I was humiliated, hearing details of conversations where Rell called me names like "Bloody Deidra". He was making jokes of it. He had more encounters with young girls after that and his ways eventually caught up with him.

Seeing my mother hurt in such a way made me realize the price I had to pay after being defiant was too expensive. My mom had me on close watch as she nursed me back to health. I was so weak; I could barely walk from losing so much blood. My heart beat rapidly as I struggled to catch my breath. She was compassionate, but very disappointed. It was extremely embarrassing for me to go out in public because everyone and their mom knew what happened and formed many opinions. I learned the hard way at a very young age and I thank God for sparing my life. Although, it wasn't easy, I did my best to earn my mother's trust back, but it took time.

I became traumatized relentlessly from that experience, which kept me from being in the hands of multiple men, due to not trusting them. After that incident I made more mistakes, including having an unwanted abortion at the age of sixteen that plagued me with more scars. I thought having a baby would fill my emptiness, but when I had to terminate the pregnancy depression consumed me. I finally found the love I was searching for in God. Reflecting back, and now realizing that God was chastening me as a way to protect me from unforeseen damage. I stopped waiting for my dad to show up, and I wiped my tears. Through having a relationship with God, He showed me how to love myself and how to establish my own worth, and my virtue was restored. I never got any answers from my dad as to what happened during that time of his absence, but today we have a better relationship. Forgiving someone who didn't know they had to be sorry, took growth. I desired to live for God and to witness His redemption.

It took God blessing me with a husband for me to see the residue of emotional and physical neglect and abandonment that I carried around and brought into my marriage. This man truly loves me and it was hard to be receptive because I never felt true love from a man. Once I realized the emotional baggage I was carrying, I was able to unload it and love my husband, as well as myself, unconditionally. He is a present father to our children because he knows how it feels to grow up having the void of an absent father. Today I share my testimony with younger girls to allow them to see where I came from and how they can prevent themselves from going down a similar road. Blaming the outcome of my actions on someone else is not practical; ultimately I had other options, but instead I chose rebellion. God covered my sin and brought me to full restoration after finding who I was in Him. My empty void was finally filled once I became aware that I actually had one. The only way to love, and respect someone, is to first love and respect you. I am not a victim; I am a victor and I walk victoriously every single day.

Deidra Jackson-Middleton Bio:

Deidra Imani Jackson- Middleton, also known as "Deige", is a prayer intercessor for the Kingdom of God and a willing servant of the Lord. She is a wife, mother, entrepreneur, first-time author and a motivational speaker and has a heart for God's people. While enjoying helping and advancing those in the community, she is an active Board member and Corporate Executive Secretary of a successful non- profit organization (Bay Point Community All-N-One). She is the Vice President of the Diamonds ministry in the Women's department at her local home church where she operates in leadership. Deidra is an aspiring life-coach and currently working towards obtaining her Bachelor's Degree in Nursing.

She was born in Monterey, CA, but was raised in Pittsburg, CA, for the majority of her life. She attended Wilberforce University in Ohio and enjoys doing hair, praise dancing, singing, praying and ministering to others, as well as, writing. Deidra has always had a passion for writing and now with two book compilations completed, she is now pursuing her first solo book project.

Currently Deidra is working as an Administrative Assistant II/ Lab Associate and also building up her faith group "Fearfully and Wonderfully Made", where she advocates the transformation of others both physically and spiritually through Christ. She has overcome many obstacles and life altering events but walks in victory only because of her encounter with God. She has been delivered from fear and anxiety, depression and low self-esteem. Today she uses her passion for writing to encourage others by the words of her testimony and by walking out her true identity, which is serving the Lord with her whole life.

"Overcomer"

By

Christina Aguilar

Author ~ Speaker ~ Aspiring Minister

www.Christinaaguilar33.wixsite.com/author

Christinaaguilar33@yahoo.com

My name is Christina Aguilar and I am 32 years old. Let me take you on a journey. I remember growing up as a child living with my mother. My father was absent from the home. My father was battling drug addiction and he lived In Los Angeles, CA. I would see him sometimes or he would write me letters, but that's about it. This was really hard for me as a little girl. I use to see other kids with their dads and I wanted that in my life. I just wanted to hear my dad say, "I love you" and "everything is going to be okay." But I never got that.

I remember being ten years old and my mother married this man that I did not like at all. Because of course, he wasn't my real dad and he was very abusive. He would beat up my mother, kick her in the face with boots, put guns to her head, and treated her like garbage. It got so bad that my mother had me put a phone in my room. She said, "Hide this just in case you have to call the police." One day he got mad, picked me up by my throat and held me in the air. I was scared. He nicknamed me "The 911 b*%#h" and that put a lot of fear in me. This created a wall around my heart so it kept me from trusting people. It was even hard for me to trust Jesus because of all the people who let me down.

"There is no fear in love, but perfect love cast out fear, because fear has not been made perfect in love." (1 John 4:18)

I got pregnant at sixteen years old. My kid's father was older than me. It was an unhealthy relationship. There was a lot of physical, emotional, and verbal abuse going on, but no love. Nine years of hell for me. The only good thing that came out of that relationship were my beautiful kids.

In 2011, I remember my life was a mess. I was doing drugs, sleeping around, drinking, and hanging out with the wrong people. That was before I went to church. My whole thinking process was a mess. I was so miserable. When I looked in the mirror I didn't love myself at all. I had so many masks on. My breaking point was one time being so drunk and hanging out with a friend that I blacked out and beat her up. I remember her grandma dropped me off at my house. I had this thought to take pills and die. So I went in my room and grabbed all the pills I could find. I took them, walked outside, called my aunt Denise and told her this, "Just want to tell you I took all these pills and I want to die." Then I remember the ambulance pulled up and they drove me to Martinez hospital. I had to drink this black stuff. Hours later, when I was sober, I talked to a doctor and told him, "I don't really want to die I'm just going through stuff." My aunt picked me up. It was about 4 am in the morning. She drove me home. I walked into the house and went straight to bed. As I went through these things, I started to feel like, "Why me?" and I started feeling like a victim.

"VICTIM FEELINGS"

Helplessness, loss of control, negative thinking, strong feelings of guilt, shame, self-blame, and depression.

When I got older, I decided to write a letter to myself as part of my healing.

"LETTER TO SELF"

DEAR CHRISTINA,

I know it was hard for you to grow up without a father. You used to see other girls with their dads and you wanted that - to be loved, protected, and that feeling of being safe. But your dad was bound to drugs, lost, confused, fighting his own inner battles. Then the day you got the news he died, you were sixteen years old and pregnant. You were shocked; you couldn't believe it. You didn't show any emotions. The day of the funeral was really hard for you. You remember walking up to the casket. Your dad looked cold and lifeless.

You were just looking at him. You got sick to your stomach and ran to bathroom and threw up. You felt like a part of you died that day. Then after his death things went downhill. You stayed in an unhealthy relationship for years out of fear. You started your drug use at the time. You made many mistakes. You were hurt, lonely, depressed, angry, insecure, and lost. You even tried to kill yourself once. You searched into the world to fill that missing feeling in your heart through people, places, and things. But it was never enough for you. But let me tell you something. You are loved, strong, and courageous. You're a good mother; you love your kids so much they are your heart. You don't need all those things you used to run to. Now you look up to God; He's your healer. He fills that missing feeling in your heart. "You can do all things through Christ who strengthens you." You're a new woman in Christ. You have a new Father; his name is Jesus. He's the best father you will ever have.

Sincerely,

I had learned many things during my healing process. I learned that if you want to become fully mature in the Lord, you must learn to love truth. Otherwise, you will always leave open a door of deception for the enemy to take what is meant to be yours. And without a challenge, there's no change.

Well, let me tell you about my life now. I'm serving God. I attend Praise Chapel in Pittsburg. I'm in the process of taking a two-year class for people who want to be pastors or missionaries. I currently have two jobs. I'm married to a loving man who treats me like a queen; he's the best. I have beautiful children who are my everything. When I look in the mirror, I love myself. I learned not to let what I have been through define me.

Before my new life, I use to cope with issues by running to the world to try to feel void. I would get high, drink, run to men, people, places, and things. But all those things made me feel empty. It was a temporary fix. The hurt, pain, rejection, and emptiness were still there. But the new way I cope with everyday life is with having a relationship with Jesus Christ; I read my bible, pray, and attend bible studies. I hang out with positive people who speak life to me and build me up to be that strong, courageous, mighty woman that I am. I put my trust in the Lord now and I have peace, joy, love, and hope. He restored my life.

When I got the opportunity to be a part of the Breaking Barriers project, I was really excited. This has been on my heart for a while. One of my dreams is to be a writer. I know this was God opening the door for me; He's so good to me. And then there were mind battles that came and of course the stupid lying devil. I pushed past fear and everything else and I stepped out on faith and trusted God. And I wanted to do this to give other women hope that even though you come from a broken past, you can find hope, joy, peace, and love in Jesus Christ. And look out for my upcoming book coming soon, God bless.

I leave you with this.

WHO am I? *(Taken from Neil T. Anderson's book, Victory Over the Darkness Pg. 45-47)*

- *I am the salt of the earth (Matthew5:13)*

- *I am the light of the world (Matthew 5:14*

- *I am a child of God (John 15:15)*

- *I am part of the true vine, a channel of Christ's life (John 15: 1-5)*

- *I am Christ friend (John 15:15)*

- *I am chosen and appointed by Christ to bear his fruit (John 15:16*

- *I am a slave of righteousness (Romans 6: 18)*

- *I am enslaved to God (Romans 6:22)*

- *I am a son of God; God is spiritually my father (Romans 8:14) Galatians 3:26, 4:6*

- *I am a joint heir with Christ, sharing his inheritance with him (Romans 8: 17)*

- *I am a temple of- a dwelling place of God. His spirit and his life dwell in me (1 Corinthians 3:16, 6:19)*

- *I am united to the lord and am one spirit with him (Corinthians 6: 17)*

- *I am a member of Christ's body (1 Corinthians 12:27)*

- *I am a new creation (2 Corinthians 5:17)*

- *I am reconciled to God and am a minister of reconciliation (2 Corinthians)*

- *I am a son of God and one in Christ (Galatians 3:2_6)*

- *I am a heir of God since I am a son of God (Galatians 4:6-7*

- *I am a saint (1 Corinthians 1:2) Ephesians 1:1) Philippians 1:1*

- *I am God's workmanship- his handiwork born anew in Christ to do his work Ephesians 2:10*

- *I am a chosen of God, holy and dearly loved (Colossians 3:12, 1 Thessalonians 1:4)*

- *I am a son of light not of darkness (2 Thessalonians 5:5)*

- *I am a holy partaker of heavenly calling (Hebrews 3:1)*

- *I am a partaker of Christ, I share in his life (Hebrews 3:14)*

- *I am one of God's living stones, being built up in Christ as a spiritual house (1 peter 2:5)*

- *I am a member of a chosen race, a royal priesthood, a holy nation, a people for God's own*

- *Possession (1 peter 2:9)10. I am an alien and a stranger to this world in which I temporarily live (1 peter 2:11)*

- *I am an enemy of the devil (1 peter 5:8)*

- *I am a child of God and I resemble Christ when he returns (1 John 3:1, 2)*

- *I am born of God, and the evil one the devil cannot touch me (1 John 5:18)*

- *I am not the great "I am " exodus 3:14) john 8:24)28, 58,) but by the grace of God, I am what I am (1Corinthians 15:10*

Christina Aguilar Bio:

Christina Aguilar is a 32 years old mother of three beautiful children. She is married to a loving man. Christina was born and raised in Pittsburg, California. Christina grew up in a single-parent home. Her father was absent from her life as he battled a drug addiction. During her childhood, Christina struggled with feeling alone especially without having her father present. Feeling alone and unloved while trying to fill her fatherless void, led Christina down a path of drug addiction and self-destruction. After her father's passing, the feeling of something missing still lingered. After years of ups and downs, Christina was invited to a church that would change her life. She gave church a chance and found out that the love she was looking for was in Jesus. She gives all thanks to Jesus for mending her broken heart and allowing her to finally move past her past by releasing the pain she held inside. She received deliverance from all addictions and strongholds that held her back in life. Being aware of everything she has been through, Christina hopes to show others that they can overcome their past and have a brighter future. Through her testimony, books, and future speaking engagements, Christina hopes to inspire others to trust and love God. Christina feels so very thankful and gives God all the Glory for the wonderful changes in her life.

Restoration - I choose to restore my life!

I am not giving up, I am starting over!

By

Tamela Sullivan

Age: 44

San Jose, CA

Co-Founder of InPowerment University ~ Mother ~ Event Planner ~ Speaker

Contact Information: Tamela04@gmail.com

My Beginning:

November 4, 1972, a baby girl came into the world and her name was Tamela Alexander. What a beautiful name for a beautiful baby. We will give her the nickname Tam. This is where my story begins. When I was a little girl I often read books instead of playing with dolls with my sister and the neighbor. Everyone thought I would become an attorney as an adult because I loved to read, but to my surprise and theirs, my life has gone a different direction.

As I began tapping into the core of who I really am, I discovered more about myself than ever before. I discovered that I am a people pleaser. I did everything to make others happy, but in the end I was the one suffering while everyone walked around with a smile. I realize I only went to college to make my parents happy. I am glad I went to college, but at the beginning it was to please my parents, especially my father. I wanted him to feel proud that I accomplished something. I stayed married longer than I should have because I did not want to let my kids down. I wanted my children to have their father in their lives 24/7 and I didn't want to be a statistic to society - another African American family ending in divorce and the children living in a one-parent household. Lastly, my nephew. My nephew and I had a close relationship, until he graduated from high school, went away to college out of state, and came back to California to live in my home. He became disrespectful and thought he no longer had to follow my rules since he was gone for a year. I put up with his actions for longer than I should have, because I did not want to hurt my mother, sister and my nephew by putting him out of the house. I always told him that I would never give up on him, but I always believed he gave up on himself. I always felt I was screaming and no one wanted to hear me until now . . .

My Dream:

"Poison, Poison, Poison." Oh yeah, get it BBD. When I grew up, I always wanted to be a BBD (Bell Biv Devoe) dancer and actress. I wanted to be in the entertainment business so I could be seen on television. When I was a junior in high school my mother and I went to Los Angeles to pursue my acting and dancing career. I auditioned for a dance part in a play and, how exciting; I made the 1st and 2nd cut. My mother looked at me and said, "Well, what do you want to do?" I said, "We need to move to Los Angeles." My mother said, "I have to work so I am not moving to Los Angeles, but you can stay here with my male friend, whom I've known since high school. But I have to go back to work." I said, "Oh, I thought you were staying here with me." She looked at me and said, "No". I said, "Well, I guess I am going home to San Jose, California to finish high school with my friends." I wish I had been vocal about what I wanted. I graduated from high school, went to

Junior College, and then later graduated from California State University Hayward with a degree in Communications. I continue to work hard to accomplish other goals and dreams, but every time I watch a movie or dancing on television, I reflect on this part of my life. In my mind, I always wondered what would've happened if I spoke up and chose my happiness and did what I wanted to do which was to be a dancer and actress. How would my life be today?

My Fairytale:

October 1992, my friend and I decided to go to Oakland, CA to meet this guy she was dating. As we stopped to use the payphone at the gas station a group of young men approached us asking our names. One particular young man stood out from the rest because he approached me directly with respect, such as saying hello, asking my name and my phone number.

This young man and I went on several dates for several months, and then low and behold, I became pregnant. I was only 20 years old. I didn't know him well enough to have his baby, so I thought about having an abortion. He convinced me to keep the child and said he would be there for me every step of the way (which he was), but I asked myself how could I raise a child when I am a child myself. I listened to him and decided to keep my baby.

January 21, 1994, I gave birth to a beautiful baby girl. Summer of 1997, he asked for my hand in marriage. August 1, 1998, I married my daughter's father. In my 25-year-old mind, I just knew I was going to spend the rest of my life with him. As years passed and another child was born, things started to change. I was growing as an individual, doing things such as traveling, growing my career, and exposing my family to the endless possibilities that God promised each of us, while my husband was complacent. My husband and I no longer spent quality couple time together, such as going to the movies, traveling, and dinner. Hell, he barely held my hand.

The year is 2008; I had a sense that my fairytale marriage was in a tailspin as I was circling the drain. I turned to my mother for marriage advice since she had experience in this area. Her first advice was to stay in my marriage, then she said, "Honey, you have a good man, try to work things out because I don't want you to end up like me divorced. And Tam what about the kids? Think about what this will do to the kids." Damn, did she have to involve the kids? What about my feelings? No one asked how I felt?

Thinking about what my mom said regarding the kids, she was right. How can I do this to them? They need their father around 24/7. I decided to take my mom's advice and work things out even though I was no longer interested in maintaining my marriage. My needs at 25 years old were different from my needs at 36 years old. Not realizing that by staying in a loveless marriage, I was showing my children it's okay to be in a marriage and compromise yourself when you are not happy. In 2009, I found my voice. I created boundaries and admitted to myself while driving home crying, finally saying the words out loud, "I am divorcing my kid's father. I don't want to be in this marriage anymore. I am unhappy. I deserve to be loved as I am giving love." How can I be there for my kids emotionally and spiritually when I don't have those things? I can't teach what I don't know or give what I don't have. It's October 2009 and I found myself at the courthouse filing divorce papers. I never thought nine years ago when I said my vows in front of God, my family and friends that I would be getting divorced. Wow Tamela, you are beginning to find your voice and stand up for yourself.

You Will Respect Me:

It was December 1994; my sister gave birth to a baby boy. I am excited to be an auntie for the first time. My nephew's father was in and out of his life, so his mother, grandmother and me, raised him. In 2003, my sister moved to Fairfield, CA,with my nephew and her baby girl. My nephew, being a nine-year-old young boy, was getting into trouble at school and with other boys in the neighborhood. My sister called me constantly complaining about my nephew's actions so I thought I would help by suggesting he come to live with me and my family. It was the summer of 2004, the beginning of his 8th grade school year. My nephew came to live with us and his actions begin to surface; he would not do his chores when asked and would not take me seriously. Now I understood what my sister was talking about.

It's now summer of 2005; I am enrolling him into high school. His actions are becoming more and more disrespectful and it's something I know longer want or should have to deal with. He doesn't make it home by curfew, he is not cleaning up behind himself, and he is not living by my house rules. He was really working my last nerve.

I threaten him several times to send him back to live with his mother, but he would always promise to do better. He apologized many times only to minimize the issues that were going on and to get back on my good side. But he would always revert back to his ways. When I spoke to his mother, she would respond, "Tam, can he stay there and finish high school?" My mom would chime in and say, "Tam, he is a kid, let him stay." I was not happy about my decision, but once again, I gave in and let them have their way. I would pray over and over to God to please give me the strength to deal with this boy. I felt alone in this fight. My sister's actions made me believe she was not interested because he was no longer in her home, and my mom just wanted him safe. I started to believe this was my battle and my family was leaving me on the battlefield to fight by myself.

It's summer of 2010, I have one more year with my nephew and he will be graduating from high school then I can hand all his issues back to his mother. It's now May 2011, whew, he graduated from high school and my job is done, so I thought. My nephew and his mother decided he would go away to college out of state. I always believed that was a bad idea because he was not mature enough and his study habits were not up to par. But who am I? I am only auntie, not mom; so he left and I was relieved. While he moved on with his college life, I felt a burden lifted off of me and I could concentrate on my children. I love my nephew, but he was a lot to deal with.

My nephew lasted a year in college and he returned back to California. I told myself I was done dealing with him and his actions. I suggested he go live with his mom so he could build a better relationship with her since he had been living with me from 8th grade through high school. That only lasted a few weeks. I was later asked if he could come back and live with me because he found a job in Oakland, CA, working at night. Looking out for his safety, his mom did not want him crossing the bridge at night to Fairfield, CA, so she thought it would be safer for him to stay in San Jose, CA. In my mind, I said, "No one ask him to find a job in Oakland; why didn't he find a job closer to his mom's house?" My mother chimed in and said, "I don't want anything to happen to him, Tam, just let him stay here and stop being mean." I didn't want anything to happen to my nephew either, so once again I gave in. I let my mom and sister make the decision for me and I allowed him to come live with me again.

The stress started again. He was doing the same things he was doing in high school, but worse. He was disrespectful, not cleaning up, eating all the food, laying clothes on the floor, and talking back. Once again, I threatened to kick him out of my house but at the request of my mother and sister, I let him stay. I remember talking with someone dear to my heart and they asked me, "Why do you put up with your nephew's actions when he has a mother?" I responded, "I put up with him in order to keep peace with my mom." Their response was, "How can you have peace when you are always at war in your home?" Wow!! This gave me something to think about. In September 2015, my nephew pulled the biggest stunt of his life, which caused me to call the police at 2:00 am in the morning. I was hurt by his actions because of everything I had done for him. I was always there when he needed me. How could he do this to me? I finally had enough and I kicked him out and I let him know he was no longer welcomed to stay in my home. Wow, it felt good to have a voice and finally be heard and be taken seriously.

My Message:

Behind this laugh and smile was a hurt little girl. When I look back at my life, I wish I had the courage inside of me to say what I felt at the time of my unhappiness. When you don't use your voice to speak your peace, you allow others to dictate your path and hold your voice hostage. For example, if I had spoken up about staying in Los Angeles to pursue my dancing and acting career, just imagine where my future would look like. Hollywood maybe? When I did not use my voice to speak up about my marriage and held on to a man whom I fell out of love with, this did nothing but make me resent the people around me and begin to give up on love. When I did not stay firm with my nephew about living with me, I allowed people to take advantage and not listen to me. I now speak my voice. I always felt I was screaming and no one could hear me, but now I am heard because I work hard to make sure I am heard and I have more confidence in myself. Because I did not speak up, it meant I gave up on me. I had to learn that I matter and what I say matters. And as long as I am happy, I cannot worry about those who I make uncomfortable about my newfound voice. But please don't mistake my confidence for being rude and heartless. You can read more about who I am, and the struggles I have overcome in my life, when my book comes out in spring of 2017. Just remember,

"Sometimes, it takes a painful experience to make us change our ways." Proverbs 20:30.

Tamela Sullivan's Bio:

Tamela was born in Oakland, CA, but raised in San Jose, CA. She is the youngest of three siblings and has many close friends in her life who she also calls her sisters. Tamela is a mother of two amazing children.

Tamela has a Bachelor of Science degree in Speech Communications from California State University Hayward, a Certification in Human Resources Management from University of California, Santa Cruz and she is currently working on her Event Planning/Meeting Management Certification from San Francisco State University. She loves to give back to her community. She enjoys volunteering for non-profit organizations, such as the Woman Battered Shelter and Family Giving Tree. She is an active volunteer for the Green Scholar Program, which helps enhance the awareness of STEM to African American Children.

Tamela Sullivan is the co-founder of INPowerment University where she helps women and young girls find the beauty and talent within themselves to feel INPowered. Her passion for helping young woman and girls stems from her own growing pains, along with the growing pains of her daughter and her daughter's friends, as she watched them transition from little girls to women. Her passion also stems from her background as a trainer at a local Credit Union. While training, she came across many women with similar growing pains as hers; such as being mentally abused by men, trying to please everyone except herself, to becoming a mother at a young age. With the many obstacles Tamela has gone though, many people doubted her, making comments such as "she would never amount to anything; will she ever finish college; and will she end up a statistic." Tamela was determined to beat the odds against her and the only way she was able to do so was by staying prayed up and keeping God first. She is sharing her story in a book compilation titled, *"Breaking through Barriers, Volume 2."*

Tamela has many goals she will accomplish from sharing her story in this book, growing INPowerement University, motivational speaking, growing her event planning business, and opening a hall that people can rent to have joyous events. As you see, Tamela Sullivan has a love for her community and helping women and young adults achieve their goals to take their dreams to the next level. One of her favorite bible verses is Philippians 4:13, "I can do all things through Christ who strengthen me."

The Take Away (Epilogue)

To end this amazing book, I thought it would be awesome to point out some words of wisdom, or messages, featured in each story. There is definitely more than one message in each story. This book features amazing women from different walks of life, each with different, impactful testimonies. In my experience, I believe wisdom is a purely internal thing as we learn lessons at all ages. But the wisdom we gain from learned lessons and the breakthroughs we accomplish, is the beauty added to the message.

"The Journey to Completing My Purpose"

Author Anita McAllister

"The moral of my story is that sometimes we make choices that we regret; we make choices to provide for our families, even if it's a choice that we're not completely comfortable with. Now I'm a totally different woman. I am completely sold out to Christ; the darkness that I was in is no longer there. I now see the light at the end of the tunnel. I praise God with all that I have because I now know that it was Him that got me through all of my dark times."

"I got my smile back and now it's legit. I'm still discovering my purpose and pursing it through Christ. No more tears, they have all dried up. No more brokenness, God has restored me and made me whole. No more walking in darkness, I now walk in the light of Jesus."

"Stepping Out On Faith"

Author Keisha Frowner

"After I had my children I had become complacent. I felt stuck in some ways and did not know how to get unstuck. There had to be more to life than going to work and coming home. There were some days of frustration. Raising my girls as a single parent was not easy. I knew I had to provide for my daughters and not make an excuse. I am starting to realize that God's timing is best. The things I went through were not wasted. What the devil meant for evil God turned it around for my good."

"I had to trust the process even when I did not know when it would happen."

"Surviving Even Though the Odds are Against Me"

Author Sherron Meadows

"I have faced many challenges in my life, but no matter what struggles came my way I decided to keep moving forward and to never look back, no matter what the cost. I have come to a point in my life where regret is no longer an option. I can only move forward from where I am today in my life and expect the best."

"I was embarrassed to share what I was really going through until I figured out that I was never alone and I told myself that I had been a fighter all my life. I can't give up when the road gets bumpy. I want to make a difference for others and help them find a better solution. If we are in a bad situation or we do not like what we are seeing in our lives, then we are the only ones that can change our situations."

"I'm Coming Out"

Author Monique McCoy

"I watched so many people walk in their purpose and live their dreams. How could I walk around with so much greatness inside of me and not share it with the world?"

"Someone once told me that in order to get to the next level in your life you have to get uncomfortable. I've been beyond uncomfortable lately. But, the beautiful thing about life is that every morning that God allows you to rise, no matter where you are in life, He gives you another chance to start over. You have to use the lessons from yesterday as a compass for the days ahead."

"Life Path"

Author Danae Braggs

"The fond awareness of her life path philosophy and her newfound eagerness to share it with those she encounters are both signs that all the choices made – bad or good – led right up to this very moment. *"All things work together for good"*. So goodbye, shoulda, woulda, coulda... Hello, woman on a mission."

"Reflecting on how you got where you are can be painful and can bring up a lot of different emotions. You have to keep in mind that without the bad you wouldn't know how good the good is. It's a necessary process for growth."

"Lessons Turned Into Blessings

Author Eshe' Satcher

"My story has just begun! I am starting to learn to change my mindset to being more positive. Since I have done this, I have been having more positive outcomes and notice that I have not been so stressed out. The moral of the story is that your past makes you who you are: Learn from your past and never give up on yourself!"

"Spiritual Warfare"

Author Andrea Taylor-McCoy

"It's been a journey. I would like to encourage you through my own personal spiritual warfare and experiences. If you have a child that's been afflicted in some way through a birth defect, sickness or disease, I would like you to know our kids were not born to be submitted to any illness, sickness or birth defect. You can choose to believe a different report, but know you will have to speak to it."

"I am not my Circumstances. It was necessary!"

Author Jamelia Jordan

"How we love ourselves sets the stage for how we love and how we receive love from others. It is hard to both give and receive love when we don't actually know what it looks like."

"The most tragic thing in the world is not death, but life without reason. It is dangerous to be alive and not know why you are given life. The enemy almost had me. He definitely played on my weakness, but my God was bigger than my struggle."

"A Banana and a Prayer"

Author Taliah Johnson

"I tell this story to encourage you. You may be thinking that what you're going through will destroy you, but God is just moving some things around! He's saying, *"Let me give you a change of scenery!"* If you are reading this and feel that all is lost, I want you to know that you are not forgotten! You will survive."

"Overcomer"

Author Christina Aguilar

"I had learned many things during my healing process. I learned that if you want to become fully mature in the Lord, you must learn to love truth. Otherwise, you will always leave open a door of deception for the enemy to take what is meant to be yours. And without a challenge, there's no change."

"I pushed past fear and everything else and I stepped out on faith and trusted God. And I wanted to do this to give other women hope that even though you come from a broken past, you can find hope, joy, peace, and love in Jesus Christ. "

"An Empty Void That Was Finally Filled"

Author Deidra Jackson-Middleton

"I finally found the love I was searching for in God. Reflecting back, and now realizing that God was chastening me as a way to protect me from unforeseen damage. I stopped waiting for my dad to show up, and I wiped my tears. Through having a relationship with God, He showed me how to love myself and how to establish my own worth, and my virtue was restored."

"Today I share my testimony with younger girls to allow them to see where I came from and how they can prevent themselves from going down a similar road. Blaming the outcome of my actions on someone else is not practical; ultimately I had other options, but instead I chose rebellion. God covered my sin and brought me to full restoration after finding who I was in Him. My empty void was finally filled once I became aware that I actually had one. The only way to love, and respect someone, is to first love and respect you. I am not a victim; I am a victor and I walk victoriously every single day."

"I am not giving up, I am starting over!"

Author Tamela Sullivan

"When you don't use your voice to speak your peace, you allow others to dictate your path and hold your voice hostage."

"I allowed people to take advantage and not listen to me. I now speak my voice. I always felt I was screaming and no one could hear me, but now I am heard because I work hard to make sure I am heard and I have more confidence in myself. Because I did not speak up, it meant I gave up on me. I had to learn that I matter and what I say matters. And as long as I am happy, I cannot worry about those who I make uncomfortable about my newfound voice."

Mindset Rehab

With Shamay Speaks

Download Shamay's

FREE

"Mindset Rehab" Audio & Workbook Today:

Visit:

https://payhip.com/b/SEXO

Or

www.ShamaySpeaks.com

BE ENCOURAGED AND TAKE CHARGE OF YOUR LIFE FOR 2017.

Tell a friend! I hope this is the first step in changing your life for the better. God Bless you on your journey!

Check out videos and more from Shamay:

www.Shamayspeaks.com

www.facebook.com/ShamaySpeaks

www.Youtube.com/ShamaySpeaks

9Quota (925) Art and Music Awards where we give recognition to various artists who contribute greatly to the art, fashion, design and music community. This compilation of talented individuals represent the rich culture of our community and shine light on the up and comers in the area. With the support of the community nominating and voting for these people they get a chance to be inspired as well as inspire others. We have been featured on BET, MTV, Vh1, the Contra Costa Times, East County Times, Mercury News, Oakland Tribune, 89.5 fm Ozcat Radio, and 106.1 KMEL. We are well respected by city officials and always comply with the wishes of the community as well as the Pittsburg Police Department.

This event is completed organized and funded by the 9Quota staff. We take pride in our unique approach in contributing to art in the community. We are fortunate enough to present this event in the historic California Theatre located in the beautiful new revived Downtown Pittsburg area. Previously we have held this event is the Lesher Center for arts in Walnut Creek California and also other locations in Brentwood and Concord. Each winner is presented with a trophy with their named engraved on it to personalize the achievement. We thank all of our supporters.

http://9quotaawards.com/

WWW.9QUOTAAWARDS.COM

Branches of Community Services

Tanicia Currie – CEO

Founder Betty Conner

communitybranches925@gmail.com

www.branchesofcommunityservices.org

(925) 709-4406 - Business Line

Tax ID #- Available upon request

Our Mission:

Our mission is to support the community by providing branches of educational support, resources, and opportunities for personal development. In fulfilling our mission, we hope to encourage the community to create a cycle of giving back to spread a message of universal community empowerment.

Speaker~ Author~Editor~Coach

"Serving steaming cups of inspiration for your soul + success"

Contact CoCo today!

www.CoCoSpeaks.net

***E-mail:* coco@cocospeaks.net**

A Little About Coco:

About 10 years ago, I was the reluctant participant at one of my husband's music ministry youth outreach events. At the time of booking, the event planner asked my husband to share a brief story and to encourage the youth in attendance. My darling husband, happily and quickly suggested me for the task instead. His reasoning was that his gifting was music and I was a teacher with a lot of experience with youth so I was "well-equipped for the assignment." I guess he saw something in me that I didn't yet see in myself – a gift for public speaking.

Since that heart-racing, knee-knocking day, I have spoken at over 100 education workshops, women's conferences, youth and community outreaches, professional trainings, business seminars and faith-based conferences and retreats.

On a personal note, I have been happily married to my husband, Fil, for 15 years. He is my armor bearer, my best friend, my calm in the storm, and my biggest supporter (& public speaking launcher!). I have been blessed with two daughters. They are the wind beneath my wings. The three of them are my greatest joy. We live outside of Sacramento, California. In my free time, I enjoy reading, weight training, and road trips.

www.KnocksmithMagazine.com

It is no surprise that much of today's media has migrated to online platforms, but there are few truly innovative visionaries who recognize that print, images, videos and music are rapidly converging. One of these leaders is Knocksmith Magazine which is bringing all of these mediums and their fans together to experience something profoundly new and unique.

Knocksmith Magazine offers a physical print magazine that is integrated with online music and video services, via QR apps, codes and giveaways. The production team behind Knocksmith Magazine has showcased some of the emerging superstars of the independent hip-hop scene. The insightful interviews are presented as videos that are accompanied by written articles and full page images. This rich, interactive media offers a 360 degree view of the artist that can't be found anywhere else in the music industry. In addition to intimate looks at rising musical artists, Knocksmith Magazine is also the platform of choice for fans to explore the music scene. The exhaustive collection of artists and music found on the Knocksmith Magazine catalogue enables fans to hear new songs, link to download sites and find similar artists. Finally, Knocksmith Magazine is a proud supporter of music lovers. Through their "Save the Record Stores" campaign, the magazine is helping to preserve an important but endangered part of the music industry. That is why Knocksmith Magazine encourages purchase of music both online and through neighborhood record stores.